Handmade Wedding

Handmade Wedding

35 HANDCRAFTED PROJECTS TO MAKE
YOUR SPECIAL DAY UNIQUE

CICO BOOKS

LONDON NEW YORK

Published in 2019 by CICO Books
An imprint of Ryland Peters & Small Ltd

20–21 Jockey's Fields   341 E 116th St
London WC1R 4BW   New York, NY 10029

www.rylandpeters.com

10 9 8 7 6 5 4 3 2 1

Projects in this book have previously appeared in *The Art of
Living with Nature* by Willow Crossley, *Handmade Wedding
Crafts* by Betty Bee, *Paper Pom-poms and other Party Decorations*
by Juliet Carr, and *Wedding Papercrafts* by Ann Brownfield
and Jane Cassini.

A CIP catalog record for this book is available from the
Library of Congress and the British Library.

ISBN: 978-1-78249-699-1

Printed in China

Project makers:
Betty Bee: pp. 38, 42, 44, 48, 87, 90, 92
Ann Brownfield and Jane Cassini pp. 10, 14, 18, 22, 28, 32,
40, 102, 104, 106, 108, 111, 114, 118
Juliet Carr pp. 25, 35, 52, 56, 59, 62, 66, 70, 74, 78, 84
Willow Crossley pp. 82, 96, 98

Editor: Marion Paull
Designer: Elizabeth Healey
Photographers: Caroline Arber, Nick Beedles,
Holly Joliffe, Emma Mitchell, Verity Welstead
Stylists: Ann Brownfield, Jane Cassini, Juliet Carr,
Willow Crossley, Nel Haynes, Luis Peral-Ananda
Illustrator (templates): Stephen Dew

In-house editor: Anna Galkina
Art director: Sally Powell
Production controller: David Hearn
Publishing manager: Penny Craig
Publisher: Cindy Richards

Contents

Introduction

Well, the first big decision is made—you're getting married!
Congratulations! Now the fun part begins—planning. Include handmade
touches and your wedding will be stylish, budget friendly, and above all
personal—you can be sure there'll never be another one like it!

Imaginative personal touches, creative
embellishments, wow-factor arrangements—these
are the things that can make all the difference
on your big day, whether you are going for a
cosy, intimate ceremony or involving a cast of
hundreds. The 35 projects in this book cover all
stages of getting married from the excitement of
planning through the day itself to reflecting on
happy memories.

You'll be surprised and delighted at what you
can do with some paper and glue, a little sparkle,
and a lot of ingenuity. Give free rein to your
creativity, hone your skills with a bone folder (an
old-fashioned but extremely useful hand tool with
a dull, rounded edge, used to make a sharp fold

or crease in paper and card), and discover your
inner crafter.

Why not tap into the creative talents of friends
and family as well? If everyone plays to their
strengths—you may be a dab hand with ribbon
(ribbon rose posy, page 92) while your best
friend may be a whizz at paper poms (page
52)—you can have fun together and be halfway
to having the décor sewn up! Your guests will be
amazed. Perhaps you're hankering after making a
beautiful, unusual keepsake? The vintage brooch
bouquet (page 87) may be the answer, and think
of the pleasure to be had collecting all those
lovely old-fashioned brooches that you'd love to
own but would probably never wear.

The invitations obviously have to be made well
in advance, but other items can be made early,
too, including mini pom cake toppers (opposite
top left, page 35), patterned confetti boxes
(page 28), and the table centerpiece (opposite
below, page 32) using old books, handwritten
letters, and sheet music (below left). Again, half
the fun is in collecting the materials. The glorious
hydrangea garland (page 82) is made with dried
flowerheads and can also be made in advance,
although better finally assembled in situ.

Let's face it, planning a wedding is not without
its stresses and strains but don't forget, all you
really need is love—and a little paper, ribbon, and
glue therapy!

CHAPTER 1

PREPARATIONS
for the BIG DAY

Ephemera Wedding Invitations

Enchantingly romantic wedding invitations are created from ephemera salvaged from Victorian and Edwardian cards—delicate filigree edgings, embossed borders, entwined initials, and exquisite watercolor cameos placed on luxurious ivory paper. Pretty vintage "finds," such as a heart-shaped locket or a miniature fan, are perfect to enhance each invitation.

Materials

300gsm hot-pressed watercolor paper

Fine utility paper or tissue paper

Cutting board

Craft knife

Metal safety ruler

Pencil

Bone folder

Ephemera papers

Vintage gold thread

Lockets and hearts

Scissors

Double-sided tape

Multi-purpose adhesive

Spray adhesive

Pen and black ink

Eraser

Optional (to deckle paper)

Water jar

Paint brush

1

With ruler, pencil, cutting board, and craft knife, measure out and cut the watercolor paper to 7⅝ x 10in (19.5 x 25cm). Use the bone folder to fold the paper in half, making a greeting card 7⅝ x 5in (19.5 x 12.5cm), with the wrong side of the paper on the inside. If possible keep any deckle edging to the front of the invitation card, for decorative effect. Alternatively, create your own deckle edge: dampen the paper edges with a paint brush dipped in water and carefully tear the damp paper against the edge of the ruler.

2

Assemble a selection of ephemera papers, such as vintage greeting cards, old postcards, and cameos. Keep to attractively colored papers that have a pleasing texture. Find vintage gold thread and a selection of gold lockets and hearts, one for each card. Vintage jewelry and ephemera can be easily found in flea markets and antique fairs. Also look out for old lettering from cards and postcards, which can be cut out and re-used.

3

Arrange a selection on the front cover of each invitation card, using a mixture of images, a gold charm, and a few cut-out letters forming the initials of the bride and groom. Use double-sided tape or adhesive to fix these to the cover. Thread a charm with the gold thread and loop it on to the card, then glue in place.

4

With ruler, pencil, cutting board, and craft knife, measure out a rectangle 7½ x 4¾in (19 x 12cm) from the watercolor paper. This will be for the written invitation. Work out the position and wording of the invitation with pencil and ruler first. This can be rubbed out when you have finished. Using pen and ink write each card, then glue into the inside back cover of the invitation card, using spray adhesive.

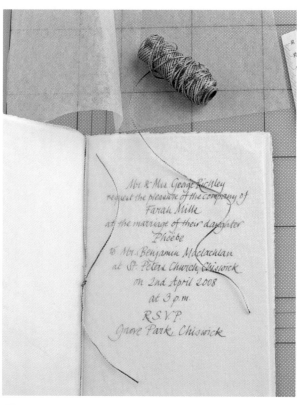

5

To fashion the lining use pencil and ruler, craft knife and cutting board to cut the fine utility paper or tissue paper to 7⅝ x 10in (19.5 x 25cm). Fold in half to 7⅝ x 5in (19.5 x 12.5cm), with the wrong side of the paper on the inside, and slip into the center of the invitation card. Tie gold thread around the spine, to hold the paper lining in place. Tie with a knot or pretty bow.

TIP Capture the pleasure of collecting intriguing paper ephemera—postcards, greetings and "calling" cards—for the delicate and tantalizing qualities of the papers, typefaces, and images used during these eras. This ephemera can be re-used enabling its distinctive character to be revealed in a fresh, contemporary way. Don't worry if a card is damaged; even a fragment or layer of filigree paper can be gently peeled away from its base—hold it in the steam of a kettle first to soften any glue. Remember, imperfections are part of their unique charm, but if a stubborn mark really bothers you, just remove it with a good-quality putty eraser.

Cutout Doves Wedding Invitations

A paper cut-out of two turtle doves entwined in leaves is reminiscent of a silhouette illustration from a children's story book. Both designs featured here make delightful wedding invitations. Inner pages of translucent paper allow the light to filter through, a nice touch that enhances the delicacy of the images.

Materials

220gsm "laid" colored paper (or similar)

90gsm Pergamenata or similar semi-translucent paper

Templates on page 122

Tracing paper

Cutting board

Craft knife with fine blade no.11

Metal safety ruler

Pencil

Putty eraser

Bone folder

Scissors

Masking tape

Spray adhesive

1

For the more detailed invitation of the two, enlarge the design on page 122 to 5½ x 7½in (14 x 19cm) and copy onto tracing paper. Use masking tape to fix the colored paper to the cutting board with the right side facing down. Working on the wrong side of the paper, measure out the invitation card to 5½ x 15in (14 x 38cm) and transfer the design to the left side of the paper using tracing paper and a pencil. Carefully cut out the negative space of the design with a craft knife. Use small strips of masking tape to hold the cut-out parts of the design to the cutting board as you cut, peeling the strips off carefully when they are not needed.

2

Cut out the invitation using the craft knife and ruler, score down the center using the bone folder and fold in half to make a card 5½ x 7½in (14 x 19cm), with the cut-out design at the front. Any pencil marks left from your trace will now be on the inside of the invitation. Remove any that bother you with a soft putty eraser.

3

For the inner lining, using pencil, ruler, craft knife, and cutting board, cut out the Pergamenata paper to 5½ x 15in (14 x 38cm), score down the center with the bone folder, and fold in half. To secure the inner lining within the invitation card, glue about ⅛in (3mm) along the folded edge of the Pergamenata paper with the spray adhesive, first masking off the surrounding areas. Tip the folded paper inside the invitation against the spine and press to fix in place.

4

For the less detailed invitation enlarge the design on page 122 to 4½ x 8in (11.5 x 20cm) and follow the previous instructions, adjusting all the paper measurements. For both invitation designs, a simple way to cut the eye is first to make a tiny cross and then cut in quarter segments.

TIP Papers in beautiful muted colors, as well as more intense hues, are stocked in art and specialist paper stores. Papers that have a pattern of ribbed lines in the finished sheet are "laid" papers—these have a matt, velvety texture and are invaluable as they give an understated elegance to any paper project. It is customary for the "laid" lines to run across the width and the "chain" lines to run head to foot—the mold used to make "laid" paper has numerous narrowly spaced wires that are woven together by very thin wires or threads called chain lines.

Decorated Table Planner

A seating plan is vital to help your guests find their table. This stylish idea of cards featuring guests' names printed in a classic italic script with flashes of gold in the hand-lettered table numbers and in the decorations of vintage buttons and earrings, is easily adapted to suit either a formal or more relaxed setting.

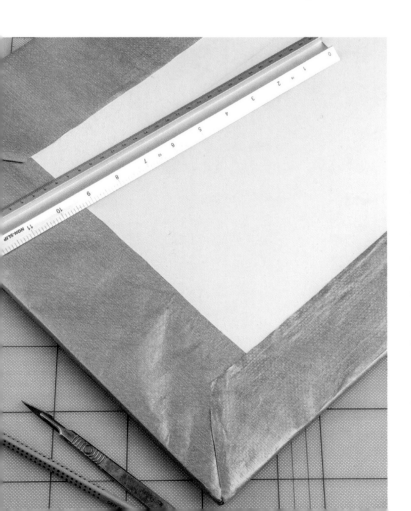

Materials

Gold polyethylene synthetic material
or gold wrapping paper

¼in (5mm) thick polyboard

Thin white card

Ivory "laid" paper suitable for computer printing

Vintage gold thread

Gold and glass buttons

Vintage braid

Vintage gold earrings

Vintage gold ribbon

Cutting board

Craft knife

Metal safety ruler

Pencil

Scissors

Double-sided tape

Adhesive tape

Spray adhesive

Multi-purpose adhesive

Gold marker pen (extra-fine point)

1

This planner has room for nine tables so increase or reduce the dimensions if you need to accommodate a different number. With pencil, ruler, craft knife, and cutting board, cut the polyboard 23½ x 15in (60 x 38cm). Then cut the gold synthetic material or wrapping paper to 30 x 21in (76 x 53cm). Glue the reverse side of the gold paper using spray adhesive, position the polyboard in the middle of the paper and press together to adhere. Turn the edges over the polyboard, folding the corners as if wrapping a parcel. Add extra adhesive if necessary. Smooth out any creases that may appear on the front.

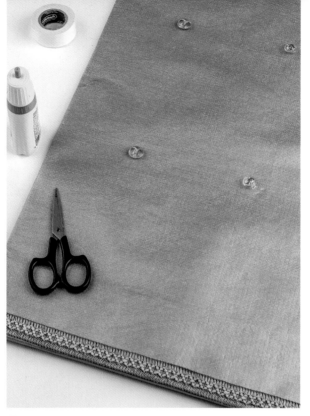

2

Cut a length of gold braid the width of the board plus approximately 1½in (4cm) each side for turning. Back this with double-sided tape. With the right side of the table planner facing you, position the trim along the bottom edge, turning the excess around to the back at each end. With pencil and ruler, measure out the position where each tag will hang and mark this by gluing on a button with multi-purpose adhesive.

3

Using the pencil, ruler, craft knife, and cutting board, cut out nine tags 4¾ x 2⅜in (12 x 6cm) from the white card. On a computer, type out a list of six guests for each tag and print on to ivory paper using a classic italic font. Cut these into 4¾ x 2⅜in (12 x 6cm) rectangles, with the names centered horizontally, leaving enough space at the bottom for the table number. Spray the reverse side of the paper with adhesive and glue each one onto a tag. At the bottom write the relevant table number with a gold marker pen.

4

To hang each tag, cut a piece of gold thread approximately 4in (10cm) long. Double this over and glue at the back of the tag, at the top edge, with adhesive tape. Decorate each tag with a gold earring simply clipped over the top edge.

5

TIP A classic script printed in black onto cream or ivory paper has a timeless appeal but to achieve a more luxurious "baroque" feel, combine with the sheen of gold or silver. Browse in local flea markets and among antique stalls and look for wooden spools of metallic embroidery thread traditionally used in *haute couture* fashion and religious or military regalia. Lengths of intricate braid and gleaming buttons are fascinating and inexpensive to collect. Vintage earrings, even if not part of a pair, are useful as they can be simply clipped onto card or paper as decoration and certainly add beguiling gleam.

To hang the table planner, or for decoration, cut a length of gold ribbon and attach it to the top edge, on the reverse side. Glue in position with double-sided tape and reinforce with a strip of gold paper if necessary. Now, hang a tag to each button starting with table number 1.

Paper-dressed Bride

A small doll, clothed in delicate papers—a petticoat of tissue, a gown of crepe, a veil of sheer Hakuryu paper—and holding the sweetest paper and pearl bouquet becomes a beautiful cake topper, or a special centerpiece for the bridesmaids' table.

Materials

7in (18cm) tall doll

White crepe paper

White tissue paper

7.5gsm Japanese Hakuryu fine white paper

White satin ribbon

Gold thread

Templates on page 124

Metal safety ruler

Pencil

Spray adhesive

Darning needle

White cotton thread

Scissors

For the flowers:

88gsm Japanese Kyoseishi bleached white paper

Green silk paper

Silver beading wire

Pearls

Thin white ribbon

Multi-purpose adhesive

Double-sided tape

Scissors

Darning needle

1

2

Using the templates on page 124 as a guide, cut out the petticoat from tissue paper, the dress from crepe paper, and the veil from sheer Hakuryu paper with scissors. Adjust the sizes to fit your doll. With needle and white thread, use tiny stitches, ½in (1cm) in from the top edge of the tissue paper, to gather the waist of the petticoat to fit the waist of your doll. Do the same with the dress but the stitches should be closer, only ⅛in (3mm) from the top edge. At the center point of the veil, as marked on the template, make four tiny pleats, close together, using the needle and white thread and tiny stitches.

Add a simple bodice of white satin ribbon around the doll and sew at the back with needle and white thread. Attach the tissue petticoat to the waist of the doll, and fasten at the back with two or three stitches. Close up the back seam with very thin strips of double-sided tape. Attach the crepe dress over the top of the petticoat, positioning it over the satin bodice. Using the needle and thread, fasten the dress at the back with two or three stitches. Use very thin strips of double-sided tape to close up the back seam. Secure the dress by winding gold thread around eight or nine times, covering the white gathered stitches, and tying in a tiny bow at the back. Attach the veil to the top of the doll's head, using a small piece of double-sided tape underneath the pleats.

3

For the bride's bouquet and headdress, cut circles from the Kyoseishi paper 1¼in (3cm) in diameter. Cut out daisy-shaped flowers from the circles. Make a hole in the center of each one with the darning needle. Cut stems from the beading wire approximately 4in (10cm) long. Thread about 1¼in (3cm) of the wire through the hole in the flower, then through a pearl, then fold back again through the pearl and through the flower.

TIP Small dolls may be found in doll and toy stores, but if you want one to a specific design and you are feeling creative, just make your own! This little doll has a head, arms, and legs fashioned from special modeling material and a body shaped from pipe cleaners, then wrapped in ribbon. The neck is a narrow piece of dowelling bought in a hobby or craft store. The modeled parts are baked in the oven and then painted using acrylic paints when completely cool. You could also experiment using papier-mâché or air-hardening clay. Keep the design of the doll extremely simple and not too realistic—her naivety is her charm. This doll would need to be propped upright so discuss a suitable way to do that with your cake-maker.

4

A spot of glue here will help secure the pearl and the flower to the wire, at the bend. Cut strips of the green silk paper about ½in (1cm) wide and 6in (15cm) long to cover each stem. Cover one side of the paper with adhesive and wind carefully around the wire stem, starting from the base of the flower and working to the end. When finished, wait until the glue has completely dried.

5

For the headdress simply make one stem into a circle to fit the bride's head, and position over the veil with the flower slightly to one side. Trim any excess wire and secure with multi-purpose adhesive. For the bouquet, gather three or four stems of flowers together and wrap with gold thread several times around the stems. Alternatively, tie them with a length of thin white ribbon and a bow.

Mini Mirror Cake Bunting

These days it's all about the detail—particularly when it comes to cake decorating. Frosting and sprinkles just aren't enough! These beautiful little bunting shimmers will add a modern touch to your cake. Small and simple, yet very, very effective. I've used mirrored card here, but any patterned card will do—just make sure that whatever you use matches your carefully planned party scheme.

Materials

(to decorate a standard 8in/20cm cake)

Template on page 125

Mirrored or patterned card

Scissors

Mini hole punch (or use scissor points and a cutting mat)

16in (40cm) narrow ribbon, ⅛in (3mm) wide, or striped baker's twine

2 long wooden skewers

Washi tape (optional)

Plasticine or modeling clay

Hot-glue gun (optional)

1
_____

Use the template on page 125 to cut five or six pennant shapes from your card.

2

Make a small hole in the top two corners of each pennant, either with your mini hole punch or scissor points.

3

Thread your ribbon or twine through the holes in each pennant so that you have a string of pennants.

4

Cut your wooden skewers to 9in (22cm) and cover with washi tape, if using. Place two small mounds of plasticine or modeling clay about 7in (18cm) apart and push a wooden skewer into each one.

5

Wrap one end of your bunting string around the top of one of the skewers, about 1in (2.5cm) from the top, and hot-glue gun it in place. Alternatively, just tie the string around the skewers. Gently lift up the other end and repeat on the second skewer.

6

Space your pennants evenly along the string and trim off any excess ribbon or twine if required. Situating them closer together will give the bunting line a deeper curve or swag. Maybe experiment before you decide exactly where you want these to go, otherwise your cake will have a few unwanted holes appearing! Then when your cake is ready, simply insert the mini bunting poles in place.

TIP This bunting is so simple to make—why not make a string of matching bunting to go around the base of your cake stand?

Materials

Selection of patterned wallpaper samples or off-cuts

⅛in (2mm) thick white mount card

20in (50cm) length of ½in (1.5cm) wide colored ribbon

Colored tissue papers

Silver ¼in (5mm) eyelet and washer kit

Small hammer

Cutting board

Craft knife

Metal safety ruler

Pencil

Compass

Hole punch

Scissors

Multi-purpose adhesive

Wallpaper: *Bovary Collection* at www.ninacampbell.com

Patterned Confetti Boxes

Cute confetti boxes of softly patterned wallpapers are punched and beribboned, and filled to the brim with tissue-paper petals. In silvers, creams, and pinks they form a harmonious array.

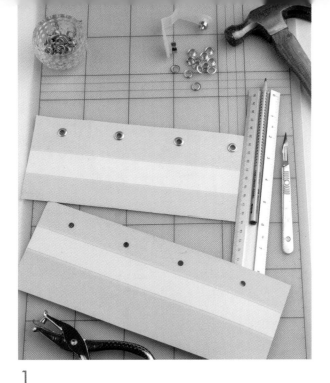

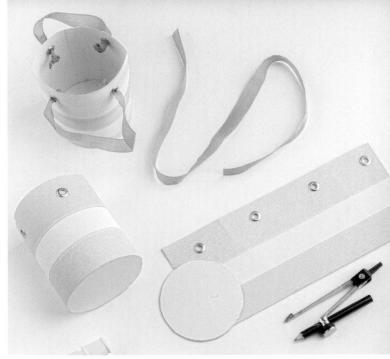

1

With ruler, pencil, craft knife, and cutting board, cut out the wallpaper to a rectangle 4 x 10¼in (10 x 26cm). Have the right side of the paper facing you and with a pencil and ruler mark four points along the rectangle for the holes, ¾in (2cm) down from the top edge. The holes should be spaced evenly when the box is completed. Punch all four holes with the hole punch. Using an eyelet and washer kit, follow the instructions given to fit an eyelet in each hole. You will need a small hammer to close the eyelets once they are in place.

2

With the compass and pencil mark a circle 3⅛in (8cm) in diameter on the card. Cut out with scissors. Apply multi-purpose adhesive along the inside edge of the wallpaper, ⅛in (2mm) from the bottom, and around the outer edge of the card circle. Wrap the wallpaper around the circle and hold in place until the adhesive is dry. Glue where the seam overlaps. Cut two lengths of ribbon 10in (25cm) long, thread each end through a hole and knot on the inside to secure.

3

For the confetti, gather together a selection of colored tissue papers to match the color of the confetti boxes. With the scissors, cut out simple heart shapes in multiples by making a wad of ten or more sheets of tissue paper and cutting through the layers. Mix up the colored heart shapes and fill each box.

CHAPTER 2

TABLE
DECORATIONS

Table Centerpiece

A charmingly original table centerpiece is created from paper leaves featuring intriguing scripts and handwriting from love notes and letters. Leaves cut from translucent papers give extra definition to the array when all are wired onto a beribboned hoop.

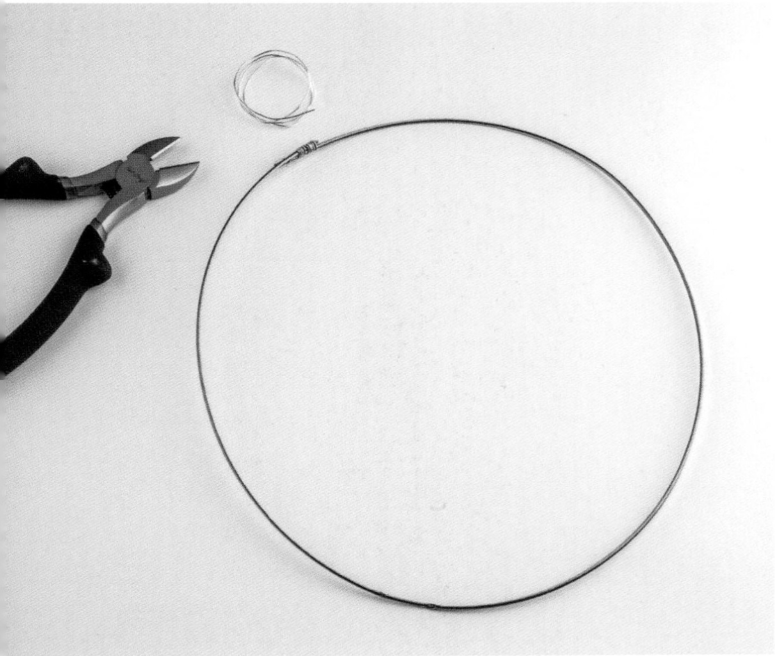

Materials

Cable wire ⅛in (3mm) diameter

Photocopied typographic papers

Translucent papers—90gsm Pergamenata, 47gsm Japanese Rayon Unryu

White ribbon 80 in (2m) length, ½in (1.5cm) wide

Templates on page 126

Wire cutters

Scissors

Double-sided tape

Adhesive tape

Silver jewelry wire

Fine gold beading wire

White acrylic paint

Fine paintbrush

Caution: Never leave a lit candle unattended and always extinguish after use

1

For the base of the centerpiece, use the wire cutters to cut a 35in (90cm) length of cable wire and twist it to form a circle. Overlap the ends of the wire by about ¾in (2cm) and secure at this point with silver jewelry wire.

2

Wrap the wire with white ribbon, having first secured it to the wire with a strip of double-sided tape. When completely covered, secure the ribbon at the end, again with double-sided tape, and trim off any excess ribbon.

3

Collect together a selection of typography from books, magazines, and handwritten love letters. Include as many decorative typefaces as you can find. Photocopy these onto white or ivory paper. From these cut out leaf shapes to a variety of sizes using the templates on page 126. Cut out more leaves from the translucent papers also using the templates. Fold each leaf down its length to give it form.

4

Gather three, four, or five leaves and bind them together at the base with a strip of adhesive tape to form a cluster. Repeat this process until you have enough clusters to encircle the entire centerpiece. Keep some leaves single to fill any gaps later.

5

To form the centerpiece, hold a cluster of leaves at its base against the wire circle and wrap tightly with gold beading wire to secure it in place. Position each cluster evenly around the wire base and secure with wire. Now adjust the leaves slightly, so that some stand up and others turn inward or outward. Disguise the gold wire with white acrylic paint.

> **TIP** A collection of old books is invaluable for sourcing intriguing typefaces, as are music manuscripts and song sheets, and letters handwritten in old-fashioned script—all these photocopy well and can be used decoratively.

Mini Pom Cake Toppers

Cupcakes are as popular as ever and there are endless ways to decorate them. These little flirty, feathery globes are a wonderful idea and when popped into the middle of a cupcake, singly or in twos, will certainly make an impression. As with many other pretty things, they can be a little fiddly to make but you can use them more than once—just make sure you snip off the end of the pop stick each time for hygiene reasons.

Materials

(makes 4 cake toppers)

1 sheet 20 x 30in (50 x 75cm) tissue paper

Template on page 125

Thin card

4 mini brads (paper fasteners)

Scissors

4 wooden skewers or cake pop sticks, 6in (15cm) long

Double-sided foam tape, ½in (1cm) wide

Decorative or colored washi tape (optional)

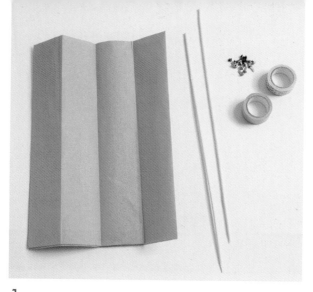

1

Fold the sheet of tissue paper in half and then into quarters, then fold again along the shortest side three times until you have a folded strip of paper about 6 x 2½in (15 x 6cm).

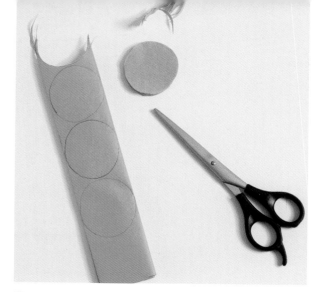

2

Use the template on page 125 to cut out a circle from the thin card. Place it on the folded tissue paper and draw around it. Repeat as many times as will fit. Carefully cut out so you have a stack of paper circles.

3

If you are worried about scattering the tissue-paper circles as you cut them, a useful tip is to make a small hole in the center of each circle before you cut them out and then push a brad (paper fastener) through each one. Open out the two pins at the back—the tissue circles are now securely fastened together.

4

Using the template as a guide, make straight cuts in the circles with the tips of your scissors, cutting from the outside edge in toward the center. Cut as close as you can to the brad. You'll find that the paper skews as you cut the straight lines, but this is fine as it helps with the feathering effect.

5

Cut a ⅝in (1.5cm) length of double-sided foam tape, peel off the backing on one side, and wrap the sticky side around the top of a wooden skewer or cake pop stick. Peel off the second layer of tape backing. Then find the central point of your paper stack and push the taped end of the stick into the middle of the layers of paper as far as it will go. Pull down three or four layers of paper over the top of the stick and gently squeeze the layers over the tape until it feels secure.

6

If you want to decorate your stick, cut a length of washi tape and wrap it around the stick, starting at the top. Alternatively, you could add one or two horizontal strips of tape to create bands of color, rather than covering the whole area.

7

Using your fingers or the end of one of your sticks, separate the layers of tissue paper to fluff up the "disc" into a ball shape. If you are posting your mini pom sticks or traveling with them, though, this is better left. Do the fluffing just before you insert the sticks into the cakes.

Materials

10oz (300g) soy wax pellets

Glass or heatproof pitcher (jug)
or measuring cup

Scented oil

Wooden skewers and elastic bands

Silicon cupcake molds

Tea-light wicks and wick sustainers

Wooden or plastic fork (the kind
you get with takeouts)

Candle glitter

Paper cupcake cases

Caution: Never leave a lit candle
unattended and always extinguish after use

Cupcake Candles

These cupcake-shaped candles make
beautiful table decorations. Of course,
they also look cute as a button placed
around your wedding cake—don't forget
they aren't edible though!

1

To make a batch of five cupcake candles, fill the pitcher (jug) to the top with wax pellets and heat in a microwave on high for approximately two minutes, or until it reaches melting point and is clear. Add a few drops of scented oil and stir them in with a wooden skewer.

2

Attach a sustainer to the end of the wick and place it in the center of your silicon mold. Pour in the wax so that it reaches the top of the mold.

3

Join two skewers at both ends with elastic bands, then thread the wick between them and rest the skewers on the mold. This keeps the wick straight as the wax sets.

4

Just before the wax sets completely, take the fork and swirl the top of the wax so that it resembles frosting. Sprinkle on some glitter and snip your wick to the desired length. Take the candles out of their molds and put them into paper cases, but always remember to remove them from these before you light them.

Feathered Bird Place Cards

A table at the wedding reception set specifically for children, with its own decorative theme and color scheme, is a lovely idea. Pretty place cards featuring cut-out doves, bluebirds, and swans, with feathered wings and tiny dangling name tags will delight every child.

Materials

220gsm (or similar) white textured paper

Tracing paper

Templates on page 123

Feathers

White silk thread

Cutting board

Craft knife

Metal safety ruler

Pencil

Bone folder

Scissors

Double-sided tape

Adhesive tape

Multi-purpose adhesive

Sample pots of matt emulsion paint (soft grays and blues)

Artist's flat paintbrush

Silver beads (for eyes)

Silver marker pen (extra fine point)

1

Using the templates on page 123 as a guide, copy the dove onto tracing paper to 6in (15cm) wide using a pencil. Cut out a rectangle of the textured paper and paint on both sides with a soft gray emulsion paint. When dry, transfer the bird image onto the painted paper. Alternatively, use colored paper in a pale gray or blue.

2

Cut out the bird using a craft knife and cutting board or scissors. To decorate the bird, glue a tiny silver bead for the eye and color the beak with silver marker pen. Attach a feather wing to the front with a spot of glue or double-sided tape. For the bluebird and swan, follow these steps, using silver paper, not pen, for the swan's beak.

3

Using the craft knife and cutting board, cut a 6¼ x 5⅛in (16 x 13cm) piece from textured paper; fold in half to make a card 3⅛ x 5⅛in (8 x 13cm), using the bone folder. Cut a 1 x 2½in (2.5 x 6.5cm) name tag from the painted paper. Cut a ¾ x 2⅜in (2 x 6cm) rectangle from the white paper and attach to the name tag with double-sided tape. Write the name on the tag. Cut 5⅝in (14cm) of silk thread, fold in two, and stick both ends to the back of the tag with adhesive tape. Loop around the bird's neck. Stick the finished bird to the card, using double-sided tape.

Lollipop Place-name Holders

Old-fashioned-candy tables have become increasingly popular at weddings over the last few years. Guests love the nostalgia of eating licorice laces and soft chews. Why not take the idea one step further and use lollipops as place-name holders?

Materials

Crepe paper in a variety of candy shades

Scissors

Hard candy lollipops

Card

PVA glue

Rectangular self-adhesive labels

Colored or metallic pens

1

Cut a piece of crepe paper approximately 12 x 8in (30 x 21cm). Place a lollipop in the center and wrap it up, twisting where the lollipop meets the stick. Tie a ribbon around the twist to secure it. Trim the top of the crepe paper so that some of the lollipop stick can be seen.

2

Cut a strip of cardboard approximately 2¾ x 1¼in (7 x 3cm). Overlap the ends and glue them together to form a circle. This will be the stand for the lollipop, so ensure the fit is snug enough for the lollipop not to fall over.

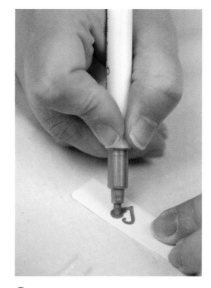

3

Cut a small rectangle from the short side of a self-adhesive label. Peel off the backing and fold the label in two lengthwise so that a strip of sticky label is exposed at one end. Use your colored or metallic pens carefully to draw a heart on the label and add your guest's name.

4

Wrap the sticky end of the label around the lollipop stick as many times as it will go, and place the lollipop in the stand. Repeat to make as many place names as required, using different colored paper for a "pick 'n' mix" effect. Position the lollipops at each place setting to help guests find their seat.

China-teacup Table Centerpiece

Make a beautiful table display using vintage china. The cups don't have to match—in fact, it can make a greater impact if they don't. However, try to tie them together with a theme (birds or flowers, for example) or with complementary colors.

Materials

Three-tier cake stand fixing

White enamel paint

Small paintbrush

Three teacups and one saucer

Tape measure

Pen

Fully charged cordless drill with a tile drill bit—this is important, as a normal drill bit will break the china

Safety goggles

Screws and washers

Screwdriver

Flowers

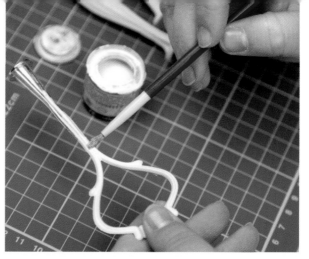

1

Paint the cake stand fixing with white paint. You can leave this gold but the white makes it look more like a whole unit with the china.

2

Make sure the saucer and teacups are clean and dry. Measure the diameter of each one and mark the center with a pen. This will act as your drill guide.

3

Time to put on the safety goggles! Find somewhere to drill the saucer and teacups where they won't slip and you won't drill into something precious underneath—a workbench is ideal.

4

Put a small amount of water in the saucer and the teacups to keep the drill bit and china cold. Slowly drill each piece through the center marking you made in step 2.

5

Assemble the cake stand, starting with the saucer. Put a washer on the base and then push the bottom screw into the saucer. Put a washer on the topside of the saucer and then fix the cake-stand fitting. Add a washer and attach the first cup, then continue until all three fixings and teacups have been attached.

6

Fill each cup with small budded flowers. The size of the cups means you can create lovely floral displays without using an awful lot of flowers—thrifty as well as beautiful.

TIP You can also use this method to make classic cake stands. Simply use a large dinner plate, a side plate, and a saucer to create the different-sized tiers.

Shot-glass Tea Lights

Tea lights are an inexpensive way to add some twinkle to your wedding and this project transforms them into something pretty enough to use as a table center.

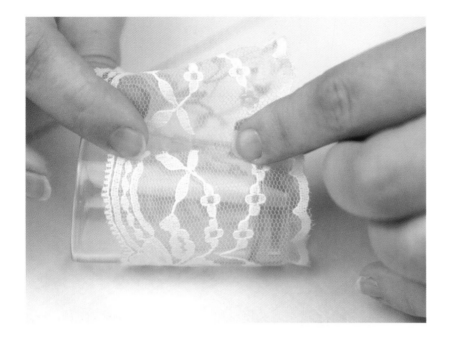

1

Measure and cut a strip of lace long enough to cover the shot glass. Stick the lace to the glass with hot glue. There is no need to put glue all over the glass—simply pull the lace tightly around the glass and apply a line of glue down the joining edge. This will create a neat seam. Glue a length of narrow ribbon around the base of the tea-light holder to make it look even prettier.

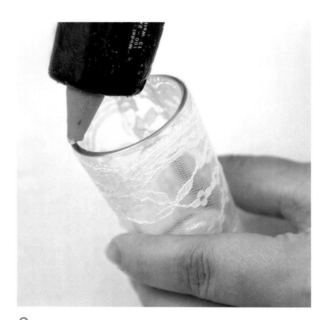

2

Take a fabric flower apart until all you are left with is the bottom petals. Sit the tea light on these and glue it in place.

3

Apply hot glue to the rim of the shot glass and place the decorated tea light on top. Repeat to make as many tea lights as required—you can make a few and group them together or place single tea lights at the center of each table.

CHAPTER 3

GARLANDS
and POMPOMS

Paper Poms

Materials

(makes 1 pom, 14in/35cm
in diameter)

8 sheets 20 x 30in (50 x 75cm)
colored tissue paper

60in (1.5m) white or colored
ribbon, ¼in (5mm) wide
(alternatively you can use
fishing line)

Scissors

Paper pompoms started out as a form of Mexican papercraft—they were paper flowers, used to adorn shrines on the Day of the Dead and for decorations at "Cinco de Mayo" (fifth of May) parties. During the 1970s, these vibrant paper flowers grew popular in the US and UK and evolved into paper poms. Fast-forward 35 years and, with the help of Martha Stewart, they are now a feature of the US bridal and party market, albeit with a modern and stylish approach. Paper poms are so versatile—they can be made in any color or size. Hang them from ceilings, beams, or curtain rails, or add them to a wall display.

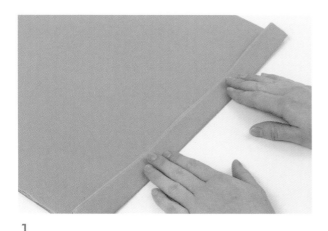

1

Lay out your eight sheets of tissue paper on top of each other and cut them in half—you should be able to use an existing fold line as a guide to cut them evenly in two. Place all the sheets together (you should now have 16 layers of paper). Starting at one of the shorter ends and keeping the stack of paper together, fold over approximately 1¼in (3.5cm).

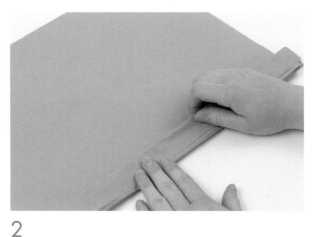

2

Turn the stack of paper over and make the next fold, using the first fold you made as a guide. Continue in this way, making concertina-style folds along the whole length of paper. Make sure the folds are even—you will soon get to know how wide 1¼in (3.5cm) is by eye! Don't worry if you end on a "half" fold, as this can simply be trimmed off.

3

Tie your length of ribbon around the middle of the pleated tissue paper to hold the folds in place.

4

Now you need to cut the ends of each fold into rounded petals. Work on just one fold at a time to make cutting easier and to stop the paper from tearing or scrunching up. Start by cutting

a diagonal line about ¼in (5mm) from one corner of the fold and make the cut about 1¼in (3.5cm) long. Use the first cut as your guide for the subsequent cuts.

5

When you have made all the diagonal cuts, start cutting the ends into rounded shapes. Pinch the top of the folds between your thumb and forefinger and use your forefinger top knuckle as a guide for the scissors to rest on.

6

Repeat steps 4 and 5 at the other end of your pleated tissue paper. Make sure your pom is even on both sides by checking the ribbon placement or by fanning open the pom and seeing if it looks unbalanced.

7

You are now ready to unfurl! Fan out both sides of the pom and pull up the first layer on either side outward and as far into the central knot as possible. If the first layer isn't pulled up into the center point, it will be difficult to open the pom into a lovely round shape and the result will be a slightly oval-shaped pom.

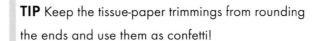

TIP Keep the tissue-paper trimmings from rounding the ends and use them as confetti!

8

Keep pulling up the layers on this first "quarter" of the pom until they are all opened out.

9

Repeat steps 7 and 8 on the opposite side.

10

Turn the pom over and repeat steps 7–9 until all the layers are open and you have a lovely, even, round ball.

Try these other pom sizes—the following all use 20 x 30in (50 x 75cm) sheets of tissue paper.

♥ For a 20in (50cm) pom: use 17 sheets. Do not fold and cut in half. Fold into concertina folds as above.

♥ For a 10in (25cm) pom: use three sheets. Fold and cut in half, then fold and cut again so that you have a stack of 12 sheets that are 10 x 15in (25 x 38cm). The concertina folds should be around ¾in (2cm) wide.

♥ For a 7in (18cm) pom: use two sheets. Fold and cut in half three times so that you end up with 16 layers of tissue paper. You will find that there are too many layers in this pom, so remove four layers, leaving 12 in the stack. The concertina folds should be around ½–¾in (1.5–2cm) wide.

♥ For a 4in (10cm) pom: use the four layers that were removed from the 7in (18cm) pom above and fold and cut in half to create eight layers. The concertina fold size should be around ¼–½in (8–10mm) wide.

♥ For a 2¾in (7cm) pom: use half a sheet, folded and cut into 16 layers that are approximately 3½ x 4in (8.5 x 10cm).

Rosette Fans

This delightful and satisfying project is so easy, and such fun to do that you could ask your bridesmaids to help you make them. Clusters of these fans can be displayed together, either suspended from ceilings or flat against a wall. Cut shapes into the ends to form petals or leave them uncut if you prefer. As you get used to the technique, you can try experimenting with wallpaper and even fabrics, such as tulle and netting.

Materials

(makes one 20in/50cm diameter rosette)

4 sheets 20 x 30in (50 x 75cm) tissue paper

Glue stick

Narrow ribbon or fishing line longer than half the diameter of the rosette (for hanging)

Scissors

Clear all-purpose glue

Colored paper clips

1

Lay two of the tissue sheets together, short end to short end. Overlap the edges by ¾in (2cm). Glue along the overlap and press down so that the paper is smooth. Make sure that the paper is fully glued down, with no gaps. Leave to dry while you repeat with the other two sheets. You should end up with two long sheets, approximately 59in (148cm) long.

2

Lay the first sheet over the second and stack neatly. Holding the two layers firmly—but not so tightly that you scrunch the paper—fold over to make a ¾in (2cm) wide crease. Then, instead of flipping over the sheets, we use the "double fold" concertina technique as follows: hold the first fold that you made (thumbs under the paper and fingers placed on top), raise the paper up toward you by around 2in (5cm) and push a similar strip under with your fingers, at the same time pulling the fold under with your thumbs in line with the first strip. Continue in this way and with each double fold that you make, press the creases down so that you form a nice, sharp, clean line. Try to keep all of the lines straight and even, as it can be easy to skew the folds.

3

Repeat until all your folds are completed. (When you get to the glued parts of the paper, you should be able to continue folding without any problems.) Tie your ribbon or fishing line around the center point and secure in place with a double knot.

4

If you find that the tissue paper is uneven at the ends of the concertina folds, all you need to do is trim them with scissors. Alternatively, cut petal shapes into the ends if desired.

5

Move the knot in the ribbon so that it is placed in the middle of the last fold. This will ensure that the rosette will hang vertically rather than horizontally. Fan out as a test to make sure that the ends meet; if they do not, re-trim at this point. Close again and run a line of clear all-purpose glue along one side of the last fold. Lay the ribbon on top of the glue—in this way it will be sandwiched between folds. This will be the top of your rosette.

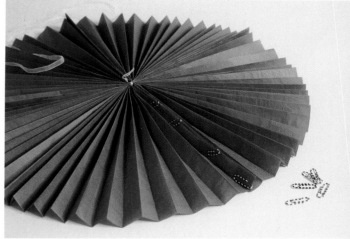

6

Fan out the top sides again until they meet, and carefully press together, encompassing the ribbon. Now fan out the bottom sides and use paper clips to secure the folds of paper at the ends of the rosette.

Hanging Pompom Heart

These romantic pastel hearts are quick to make, as there are no petals to cut and you can use a relatively small heart shape made from corrugated card. You can also buy 3-D heart shapes ready to decorate from craft stores, or you could even attach poms to a willow or hazel heart found in garden centers and home stores.

Materials

Template on page 125

Corrugated card

Cutting board and craft knife

Narrow ribbon, for hanging

96in (240cm) florist's wire

Wire cutters

4 sheets 20 x 30in (50 x 75cm) tissue paper
(1 sheet of paper will make 4 poms)

Scissors

Clear all-purpose glue or hot-glue gun

1

Use the template on page 125 to draw a heart shape on your corrugated card. Cut out the heart shape, using a cutting board and craft knife, and then cut out the middle section, so that you have a slim frame to work with.

2

Make a small hole at the top of the heart and thread your narrow hanging ribbon through the hole. Tie to secure.

3

Cut the florist's wire into 16 equal 6in (15cm) pieces with wire cutters and set to one side. Working with a couple of sheets of tissue paper at a time, fold, crease, and cut the tissue into smaller rectangles of 3½ x 5in (9 x 12.5cm), keeping your edges straight and neat. Count out eight small rectangless into 16 separate neat piles of paper. Take one stack of tissue paper sheets and fold over ½in (1cm) along the shortest length. Continue making concertina folds until you get to the end of the tissue paper. Then wrap a piece of florist's wire around the center of the fold. Twist to secure. Repeat to make 16 poms in total.

4

Fluff the poms. Hold the pom at the place where the wire is twisted (this will be the back). Tease out the first layer that is facing you. Pull this as far as you can toward the center of the pom. Repeat on the other side. Then tease and fluff up the remaining layers, all of them away from the back of the pom. Trim any long pieces of wire with wire cutters.

5

Take one pom and glue it to the "dip" in the heart shape, using clear all-purpose glue or a hot-glue gun. Continue adding poms, bearing in mind that you will need an equal amount on each side of the heart.

6

Fluff up any layers that may have been flattened. Your heart is now ready to display.

TIP If both sides of the heart are likely to be seen, make double the amount of poms so that you can attach them to the back of the heart, too.

Cupcake Flowers

Materials

Paper cupcake cases in assorted colors and sizes (2–3 liners for each bulb)

Scissors

Craft knife and cutting board

String of fairy lights

Loom bands

Buy a selection of cupcake cases, add a spare set of fairy lights and a handful of loom bands and you can create a cheery garland. If you already have white cupcake cases, simply paint or dye them with tea or food coloring to make a "one of a kind" festoon. Patterned cases are great to use, as the print will show through on both sides when the lights are on. Try mixing plain and patterned cases together for extra effect.

1

To make the main flower: take one of your larger cases and fold it in half. Fold it in half again twice until you have a cone shape, and then cut round petal shapes from one end. When the case is opened out, you should have an eight-petal flower.

2

A 16-petal flower is made in the same way, except the case is folded into sixteenths. You can also create different effects by cutting pointed petals instead of rounded ones.

3

To make the outer leaves of the flower, take a large case—preferably green in color—and fold it twice before cutting pointed shapes into it. This will give you four pointed leaves. Keep going until you have enough flower cases to fit to your fairy lights.

4

Carefully cut a cross in the center of each paper case using your craft knife and cutting board. This will allow the cases to slip over the fairy lights.

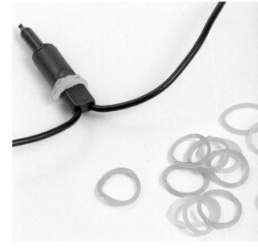

5

Tie a loom band around the base of each fairy light. Then gently push your newly cut cupcake cases over the bulb until they rest against the loom band.

6

Arrange the cupcake cases as you want them and then add another loom band around the base of the fairy lights inside the cases to stop them from moving.

TIP Rip or tear the petals, rather than cutting, to give these little light shades a boho look.

Tassel Garland

Materials

(makes 1 garland, 2¾yd/2.5m long)

10 sheets 20 x 30in (50 x 75cm) gold tissue paper

Cutting board

Rotary cutter

Wooden skewer or cake pop stick, approximately 8in (20cm long)

2¾yd (2.5m) ribbon or lace, ¾in (2cm) wide

Masking tape

Simple tissue strips and twists transform flat sheets of tissue paper into full, elegant tassels. This whimsical decoration trend started in the US as an alternative to tissue-paper poms and has become a firm favorite. The colors that you choose make all the difference to the overall effect—hot pinks, blues, and yellows give a real carnival vibe, whereas muted pastel tones make an elegant garland with a "vintage" feel. The great thing about these garlands is that you can make them as long or as short as you need. Try criss-crossing the garlands across your wedding room or marquee, or hang them against a flat surface, or simply tie them around the backs of your dining chairs for a celebratory look.

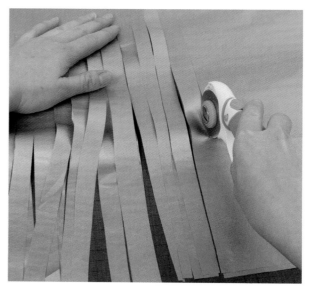

1

Take a sheet of tissue paper and fold it in half (short end to short end). Place on your cutting board and use the rotary cutter to cut vertical strips 2½in (6cm) from the fold line and ½in (1cm) apart. If your cutting mat has guidelines, you may find it easier and safer to follow these.

2

Continue along the sheet until you reach the end of the paper and then cut the paper vertically into two equal sections. Repeat steps 1 and 2 with the remaining nine sheets of tissue paper. Once you have got used to the technique, try laying several sheets of paper together before you cut to help speed things up. You should now have 20 pieces of fringing.

3

Take one of the pieces and open it out with the uncut center section in front of you. Tightly fold the center section into ¼in (5mm) folds. Repeat with all the pieces of fringing.

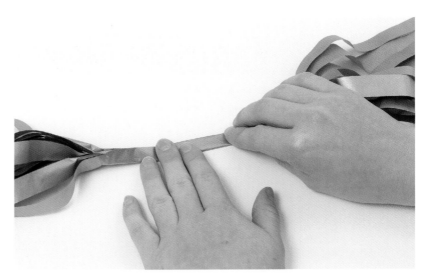

4

To create a loop in the tassel, fold the center section of the tassel over the skewer or stick and twist the paper firmly until the center section is twisted and you have a loop at the top. Repeat for all the tassels.

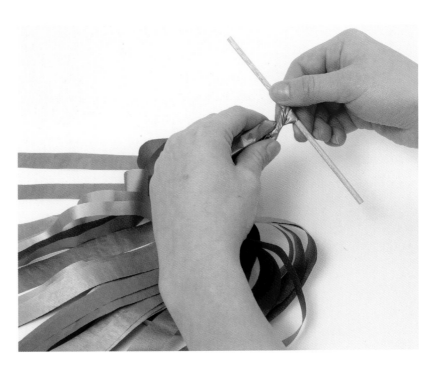

5

Finally, thread the tassels onto your ribbon or lace. The easiest way to do this is to attach the end of your ribbon to one end of your skewer or stick with some masking tape—like a giant needle and thread. Feed the stick and ribbon through the loop on each tassel until they are all on the ribbon.

6

To arrange your tassels, simply push them along the ribbon so that there is a gap of approximately 4in (10cm) between each one.

TIP Why not use sheets of tissue paper that you may have stashed away from clothes or gift packaging? For best results when using folded sheets, iron them flat before you start, using a low heat setting and no steam.

Rose Garland

There is something rather special about the spiraling pattern of a rose. This beautiful garland has roses made from coffee-filter petals, creating a whimsical and romantic rose with a retro feel. This garland is perfect for a wedding—it can be tied around the bride and groom's chairs at the reception, or draped around tables or staircases. Smaller versions would also make perfect bridesmaids' headdresses.

Materials

26 white or unbleached coffee filters, 8in (20cm) in diameter

Rubber gloves

Selection of food colorings (red, orange, yellow, and green)

Bowls or plastic pots for the dyes

Scissors

Templates on page 125

Wooden skewers

Hot-glue gun

Garden clippers (secateurs)

3¼yd (3m) seagrass twine

4¼yd (4m) florist's wire

Tape

1

Start by dividing up your coffee filters. Set aside two coffee filters to be dyed green for the leaves and then divide the rest equally between your chosen colors. Wear rubber gloves to protect your hands and then mix up your food-coloring dyes according to manufacturer's instructions, making some more diluted colors too. Dip your filters into the dyes—pinks, oranges, and yellows for the roses, and green for the leaves. Wring them out and allow to dry. Experiment by adding splatters of the same color in a darker shade to some of your filter papers.

2

When the coffee filters are dry, use the template on page 125 to cut 12 petal shapes for each flower. You can fold a few filters together to cut several petals at once. Fold the green-dyed coffee filters in half and use the leaf template on page 125 to cut three leaves for each flower, plus a few extra to add along the twine to fill any gaps between flowers.

3

Make up the flowers, starting with the center of the rose. Add a dab of glue to the end of a wooden skewer with the hot-glue gun, and roll one of the petals around it, twisting the petal to cover the end of the skewer.

4

Continue adding petals, rolling each one around the skewer and gluing it in place. Fluff the petals outward to make the flowers wider.

5

Use garden clippers or sharp scissors to snip off the end of the skewer at the base of the flower and then repeat steps 3–4 to make 24 flowers

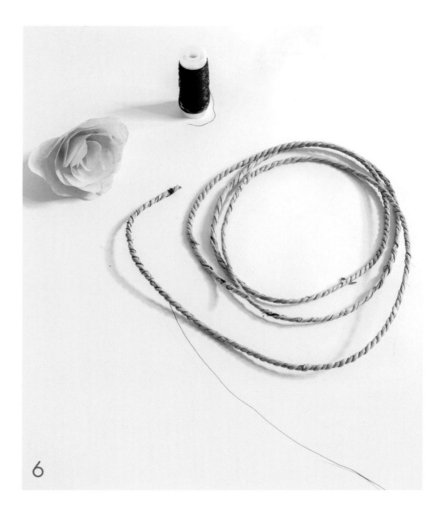

6

Wrap the end of your florist's wire several times around one end of the twine and secure it in place with a drop of glue from the hot-glue gun. Start twisting the wire tightly around the twine at an angle until you get to the end of your twine. Wind the wire tightly around the end of the line and hot-glue gun it in place.

6

7

To assemble the garland, mark sections along the line every 5in (12.5cm) with a small piece of tape. Take one of your flowers and hot glue it to the twine and wire rope that you have made. Repeat this every 5in (12.5cm) along the twine. Glue three leaves around the base of each flower to hide the glue and add more leaves to the twine between each flower.

TO MAKE A HEADDRESS You will need eight or nine flowers, 1yd (1m) of florist's wire, and 24in (60cm) of seagrass twine. Follow step 6 to make a wire and twine line that will fit around your head. Overlap the ends by 4in (10cm) and secure with florist's wire. Cover the ends of the wire with leaves. Attach flowers and leaves as in step 7.

Coffee-filter Wreath

Coffee filters have a lovely soft texture to them, while still being robust and very flexible—and, being filters, they are very absorbent, which helps when dyeing them with your own colors. The color palette here is a light mix of neutrals and pale pinks, with a few greens for the leaves. This project has to be made in several stages that each need a few hours. The dyed filters need a drying time of around four hours, as does the wreath base.

Materials

Several packs of coffee filters, 6–8in (15–20cm) in diameter—you'll need at least 130, including 10 bleached (white) filters

Food coloring in pink, orange, and green

Tea bags

5 bowls or pots for mixing dyes

Rubber gloves

4ft (1.2m) length of foam pipe insulation (available at any hardware store)

Scissors

Duct tape

Several sheets of neutral tissue paper

PVA glue

Masking tape

Stapler

Hot-glue gun

Template on page 120

1

Prepare your five dyes: light pink, dark pink, orange, brown, and green. For the two pink dyes, orange, and green, add a few drops of food coloring to a small bowl of water—add more drops for the darker pink. For the brown dye, add two or three tea bags to a small bowl of boiling water. Allow to cool and remove the tea bags before using the liquid.

2

Set aside the 10 bleached filters, then divide up the rest into 70 for pink, 40 for neutrals, and 10 for greens. Wearing rubber gloves to protect your hands, dip your filters into your mixes so that they are submerged and will absorb the colors. Wring them out and then peg them onto a line or lay them over radiators to dry. This will take a few hours.

3

In the meantime, the wreath base can be made. Use scissors to cut two rectangles of foam away from one end of the foam pipe insulation. Cut corresponding pieces from the other end, so that the two ends will fit together in a sort of dovetail joint. Place the two ends of the pipe together and tape securely with duct tape. You will now have a lovely round wreath base.

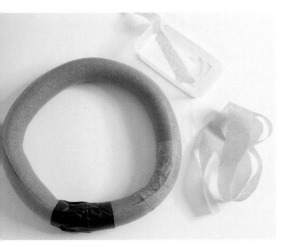

4

Tear up enough strips of tissue paper to cover the wreath base completely and paste them to the wreath base using PVA glue. Allow to dry—this could take up to four hours, but you can speed up the process with a hairdryer.

5

When your filters are dry, start making the ruffled flowers. Stack five filters on top of each other (three dark and two light), and then fold them into quarters.

6

Use scissors to cut scalloped or pointed petals into the ends. Staple the fold at the base to secure.

7

Holding the stapled end, pinch and twist the base of the flower as you open out the layers. This will create a very pretty ruffled flower. When all the layers are fluffed out, tape the base of the flower with masking tape to hold it in place until it is glued to the wreath. Repeat to create nine flowers like this, using a mix of pink, brown, and white filters.

8

To make the remainder of the flowers, place three filters one on top of the other (use graduated colors or a mix) and fold into quarters. Cut a scalloped edge along the top and then cut out the center, again with a scalloped edge. Set the outer pieces aside to use in step 9. Repeat to make about 20–30 flower centers, depending on how full you want your wreath to be.

9

Twist each flower center piece at the base to create a petal and press two or three of these onto a strip of masking tape about 10in (25cm) long. Then take the reserved outer pieces and almost pleat these as you stick them down, creating a long ruffle on the tape.

10

Take your ruffled strip and start to roll the tape from where the center petals are. This will create a shallow ruffled rose that look as though it has opened out.

11

Repeat to make 10–15 of these flowers.

13

Now start attaching your flowers—a hot-glue gun is essential here. You could cluster the larger flowers together to create an asymmetric display or literally "pick and stick." Use the smaller flowers around the larger ones and fill in the gaps with the leaves.

12

To make the leaves, use the template on page 120. Cut six or seven spiky leaf shapes from each green filter. These leaves will be glued into your wreath along with the flowers.

TIP Attach fake berries and fruit to the wreath for a spring or summer display, or icy blue and silver berries and leaves for a winter look.

Tissue Bauble Heart

This outright showstopper is easier to make than you may think. Choose brightly colored tissue paper for an even more eye-catching display. Each "bauble" is made by pressing scrunched-up tissue paper into a small glass tea-light holder, or similar small container, to mold it into shape. When they are all glued to the heart, they look remarkably like those colorful mini macarons that you see in fabulous cake shops, or wrapped chocolates. You may find your guests surreptitiously trying to eat them!

Materials

Several sheets of tissue paper in 2 colors

Scissors

Mold for bauble—tea-light holder, egg cup, or small glass pot

Template on page 127

20 x 20in (50 x 50cm) square of thick cardstock or corrugated card

Craft knife (optional)

Hot-glue gun

1

If you are using large sheets of tissue paper, cut them in half. You will need about 30 pieces of tissue paper in each color, approximately 20 x 15in (50 x 38cm).

2

Take a sheet of tissue paper and use your hands to scrunch it up into a small ball, leaving one corner of the sheet unscrunched.

3

Push the ball into the mold to get a nice round shape, then take it out and wrap the unscrunched paper neatly around the ball. Push back into the mold as firmly as you can and hold it there for a few moments.

4

When you remove the bauble from the mold, you will find it puffs out a little—this is fine. Repeat to make 30 baubles in each color (to cover the heart).

5

Use the template on page 127 to cut out a heart shape from the card, using scissors or a craft knife. If you like the natural color of the card showing through, leave it, but you can of course paint or cover the card in paper first. Use a hot-glue gun to stick the baubles to the card, starting with the outer edge of the heart.

6

Continue adding baubles, alternating your two colors as you go. (Another idea would be to use a selection of colors, graduating from dark to light.) Repeat until the surface of the card is fully covered. You may want to lay all your baubles out in position before glueing to make sure they fit.

CHAPTER 4

FLOWERS and BOUQUETS

Hydrangea Garland

Hydrangeas are a wonderful choice for decorating your wedding room, the church, marquee, tables. Garlands of these spectacular blooms in greeny-blue interspersed with pink and creamy white make a glorious feature in any venue. As well as their obvious beauty, the hydrangeas' generous size makes them doubly useful and lets you create something bold with just a few giant blooms. Dried hydrangea heads are used in this project, for convenience, but fresh blooms would work just as well.

Materials

Green ribbon or string

Copper beech leaves

Oak leaves

Strong florist's wire

Hydrangea stems

Rhododendron stems

Sprigs of rosemary, preferably in flower

Garden clippers (secateurs)

Scissors

1

Measure how long you want the garland to be with some ribbon or string. Add an extra 8in (20cm) on each end to use as hanging loops. Lay out the foliage along the ribbon.

2

Hold the florist's wire tightly and, starting at one end of the line, carefully wrap it up and around the foliage and ribbon to bind them together. Secure the wire at the other end.

3

Feed in the hydrangea, rhododendron, and rosemary along the garland wherever you want them. Depending on where the garland is to be displayed, it may be easier to hang up the line of foliage first and then add the flowers along its length. In this way, less of the garland is likely to come adrift when you hang it in position.

TIP When laying out the foliage, think of it as like a long, fat sausage, and the fatter you can make it the better—but there are no hard-and-fast rules for making this project.

Giant Rose

Roses are the ultimate romantic flower and the gesture of giving a rose is symbolic of showing great love and affection. These giant roses are perfect for your wedding day—a beautiful giant pink rose says "I love you" in a very special way.

Materials

(makes 1 rose, 12in (30cm) in diameter)

For the leaves

Plastic wrap (cling film)

Masking tape

Small bowl

PVA glue

Soft paintbrush

2 sheets 12 x 16in (30 x 42cm) olive green tissue paper

Template on page 125

Scissors

For the rose

Template on page 124

½ x 2¾yd (2.5m) roll Italian crepe paper

Florist's tape in olive or moss green

1yd (90cm) bamboo garden cane, ¼in (5mm) in diameter

Candle

Masking tape

1

2

Lay a large sheet of plastic wrap (cling film) on your work surface, securing it with masking tape. Pour 1 cup (250ml) PVA glue into a bowl and dilute with a tablespoon of water. Lay a sheet of tissue paper on the plastic wrap and brush with glue up to the edges. Immediately lay a second sheet of tissue paper over the top, guiding it with your hands. The glue should soak through. Quickly peel the paper off the plastic wrap and hang to dry for about four hours. Then use the template on page 125 to cut out three leaves.

Use the template on page 124 to cut 15 heart-shaped petals from the crepe paper, positioning the heart template over a fold in the paper. Then create a template for teardrop-shaped petals by cutting along the dotted line on the template. Cut three teardrop-shaped petals.

3

The petals are all quite slim looking and need to be stretched carefully. Do this by smoothing the petals over a smooth, round object, or your knee, to create a cupped dome shape. For larger petals use a big ball (make sure it is clean and dry!) or a melon. Don't stretch out the tips of the hearts at this point.

4

Attach your first central teardrop-shaped petal to one end of the bamboo cane by wrapping it tightly around the cane.

5

Use florist's tape to hold the petal in place. As you stretch the florist's tape and wind it around the base of the petal and top of the cane, it releases an adhesive, which bonds your petal to the bamboo cane. Apply the second and third teardrop petals, making sure that they overlap at the bottom while remaining level at the top. You should end up with something that looks like a tulip or lily.

6

Now start applying your heart-shaped petals. These should all overlap each other, so make sure when you position them that each petal covers at least half of the one applied before, so that there are no gaps in the flower. Work around the flower in the same direction until all the petals are firmly attached. If your tape breaks while you are winding and pulling, simply overlap the torn piece of tape by around ½in (1cm) with a new piece of tape and hold down firmly.

7

Attach your three green leaves using the same method as the rose petals. When you have added the final green leaf, continue winding the tape evenly down the cane. You should be able to roll the cane in your hand while pulling the tape at the same time. Roll the tape around the bottom of the cane and up again, then snip off the end of the tape.

8

To curl the petals, wrap a 1in (2.5cm) candle with masking tape and then roll the tips of the petals around the candle. Pull around and down, stretching the crepe paper as you go. Repeat for all the petals. Display in a large, tall vase or hang over a doorway using ribbons.

TIP To make a larger rose, the instructions are the same: simply enlarge the petal and leaf templates by 200%. You will need a whole roll of crepe paper and a bamboo cane that is approximately 2yd (1.8m) high and ½in (1.5cm) in diameter.

Vintage Brooch Bouquet

This is a beautiful alternative to real flowers—you can keep the brooch bouquet for ever and it is perfect for incorporating "something old, something new" into your wedding. Collecting the brooches from thrift stores or flea markets may take time, so this is a lovely project to start as soon as you have set your wedding date.

Materials

Plastic posy holder

Large oasis floral foam ball

Strong tape

½yd (½m) fabric to cover the oasis, such as a white silk mix

Garden wire—strong enough to hold the brooch but bendable

Scissors or pliers to cut wire

Brooches—for a large bouquet you will need about 40

Hot-glue gun

Craft knife or scalpel

Skewer or chopstick

Masking tape

Ribbon

Feathers

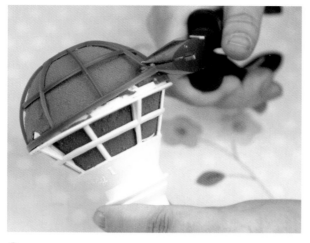

1

Remove the plastic cage and small ball of oasis from your posy holder. Tape the bigger oasis ball onto the handle using strong tape. Cut the end off your posy holder stem with a pair of scissors.

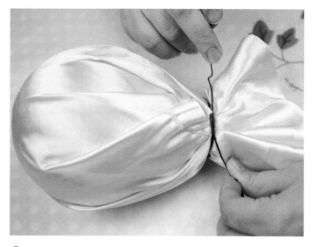

2

Cover the oasis ball with the silk fabric, smoothing it flat. Wrap a length of garden wire around the fabric at the top of the handle to secure and then trim the excess fabric.

3

For each brooch cut a length of wire the full length of the bouquet and then half again. Hot glue the brooch clasps shut. Twist the precut wire onto the back of the clasp and wind it around a few times so it is secure. Repeat this process for all the brooches.

4

Make a small hole through the fabric-covered oasis ball with a craft knife or scalpel, or a small pair of scissors. Use masking tape to stick the end of the brooch wire to the end of a skewer. Poke the skewer through the ready-made hole and then push it all the way down the stem of the posy holder. When you can see the bottom of the skewer poking out, remove the masking tape and pull the wire through. Hold onto the end of the wire while you pull the skewer out.

5

Pull the wire up over the posy handle and wrap it around the neck of the bouquet to secure it. Repeat steps 4 and 5 until the whole oasis ball is covered in brooches. Tape the wires firmly to the stem so they are flush and neat.

6

Glue a piece of ribbon to the end of the posy holder to cover it and then wrap ribbon up the stem, securing with glue as you go. Take the ribbon up the whole handle to cover all the wires.

7

Spot-glue the brooches so the whole bouquet feels really secure. Stick feathers in any little gaps between the brooches and finish with a contrasting bow.

Butterfly Bouquet

Butterflies, with their delicate wings and beautiful colors, are a lovely theme for a wedding, particularly a spring or summer wedding. This bouquet is made to look as if the bride is holding a posy full of butterflies ready to fly away. It's very light, so perfect if you don't want to hold something heavy all day. You can extend the theme to your table centers, too, by following the same steps and placing the butterfly posies in simple glass vases.

Materials

Feather butterflies, about 20

Jewelry wire

Small pair of scissors

Hot-glue gun

Pipe cleaners

20in (50cm) ribbon

Decorative pins

1

Use the point of the scissors to make a small hole in the back of each butterfly. Cut a 16in (40cm) length of jewelry wire for each butterfly. Dab a few drops of hot glue into the hole you have made.

2

Put one end of the wire into the hole in the back of the butterfly and press it down, using the end of a pencil or craft tool (not your fingers—the glue is hot!) to ensure it is really secure.

3

Once you have about 20 butterflies, gather the jewelry-wire stems together and tie them tightly with some more jewelry wire to make a single stem.

4

Now wrap some pipe cleaners around the single metal-wire stem. This will make it look more substantial and it will also be more comfortable to hold.

5

Wrap ribbon tightly from the bottom of the stem up to the top—dab hot glue at the start and end, and at regular intervals on the underside of the ribbon to secure it in place. Push a few decorative pins in along the stem.

6

Tie a bow at the top of the posy with a length of ribbon and secure it with a decorative pin. Glue a single butterfly underneath the bow to give the posy the finishing touch.

Ribbon-rose Posy

There can be few more satisfying wedding crafts than ribbon roses. After a little practice it takes a matter of minutes to make them and they have so many uses—add them to corsages and dresses, or make beautiful table centers. These posies are particularly good for flower girls and bridesmaids as they are very light to carry.

Materials

Approx 3¼yd (3m) satin ribbon for roses—the width of the ribbon will determine the size of your roses; 1¼in (3cm) wide ribbon is used here

Hot-glue gun

Plastic flower stems or covered pipe cleaners

Extra ribbon for bow

1

Cut a length of ribbon about 8in (20cm) long. Tie a knot approximately 1½in (4cm) from the end of your ribbon, so that you leave a short "tail" hanging down.

2

Holding on to the knot, fold the long length of ribbon inward and around above the knot three times. This will create your inner rose bud. Secure the bud with a dot of hot glue.

3

Keeping hold of the bottom of your inner rose bud, bring the ribbon up on a diagonal (fold it up and across) and wrap it around the bud once. Repeat this action to create folds of ribbon that resemble petals. Every time you wrap the ribbon around, use a dot of hot glue to secure it. How tightly you wrap the ribbon will affect the size and shape of your rose. As you make a few, you can decide on your preferred shape.

4

Once you have reached the end of the ribbon, glue it neatly underneath the rose.

5

Take a pair of small scissors and gently poke the inside of your flower so it all sits tightly.

6

Take your plastic stem or pipe cleaner and dot hot glue on the end. Gently push this through the bottom of your rose until it is about halfway inside.

7

Wrap the ribbon tail around the top of the stem and stick it down with hot glue. Repeat these steps until you have at least 15 roses.

Tie them together using a length of ribbon, finished with a suitable bow. Now your ribbon posy is complete and ready to go.

TIP You can use this technique to create matching buttonholes for your groom and ushers. Simply cut the stem quite short and use the ribbon tail to cover it completely. This gives you something to anchor the pin into from the back of the lapel.

Materials

Large pitcher or jug

Queen Anne's lace (cow parsley)

Lilac

Garden clippers (secateurs)

Cow Parsley

Queen Anne's lace, or cow parsley, a small, umbrella-shaped wildflower, emerges from the hedgerows in late spring like clouds of cream lace, and continues flowering for months. Sprays of these make an unusual and delicate addition to your wedding flowers.

A huge bunch of Queen Anne's lace will look ravishing on its own in a vase, but it is just as beautiful paired with lilac, as shown here, which flowers at the same time. Late-flowering white narcissi, tulips, and alliums also make beautiful companions. Pitchers and bottles provide unusual containers, and glass vases filled with shorter individual stems highlight the flowers' frothy, relaxed nature to perfection.

TIP If you dip the stems into boiling water, then plunge them into cold water up to their necks for 10 minutes, Queen Anne's lace can last for a surprisingly long time.

Dazzle with Anemones

Materials

White anemones with purple centers

Dark purple ranunculus

White ranunculus

Alchemilla mollis

Solomon's seal

Garden clippers (secateurs)

Small containers, such as narrow-necked glass jars

Larger ceramic pots in muted colors

Anemones are ridiculously pretty, so wispy and fragile with their paint-box silk petals and frilly leaves. They come in all shades of pink, blue, crimson, purple, scarlet, and white. There are three varieties that flower in spring, summer, and fall, so you can find them for most of the year. They are deceptively strong—you just need to be careful not to bash them about because their petals can tear or become stained by specks of pollen.

Here, white anemones with purple centers are mixed with dark purple and cream ranunculus, to keep the colors quite restrained. Fillers are *Alchemilla mollis* for greenness and Solomon's seal for a contrasting leaf shape.

Anemones are quite an extravagance to buy, but one way to eke them out while still creating a dazzling display is to line them up in individual containers. Try using traditional milk bottles, mini jam jars, test tubes, or vintage shot glasses.

1

Cut the stems of all the flowers on the diagonal.

2

Fill the containers with water.

3

Arrange groups of all the flowers in the large ceramic pots and reserve one or two for the small glass jars.

TIP Anemones will last about six to eight days in a vase, and you can help them along by removing any leaves below the water line. They are very thirsty flowers, so check their water levels frequently.

CHAPTER 5

KEEPSAKES
and FAVORS

Materials

220gsm white card

White crepe paper

Colored photocopies

Lilac tissue paper

Floristry wire or store-bought stems

Gold doily paper

Cutting board

Craft knife

Metal safety ruler

Pencil

Scissors

Double-sided tape

Vintage gold thread

Darning needle

Multi-purpose adhesive

Bonbon Crackers

These sweetest of crackers are made from pure white crepe paper decorated with a glint of gold doily edging, a floral band, and fragile flowers of tissue paper. Pile them on a silver tray to delight your guests.

1

To make the inner tube, cut thin white card to 3½ x 5½in (9 x 14cm) and curve into a tube. Overlap by ⅜in (1cm) and secure with double-sided tape. Cut a length of white crepe paper 10 x 20in (25 x 50cm) and two thin strips of gold doily paper, using only the scalloped edge, each one about 8in (20cm) long. With narrow strips of double-sided tape, stick the gold strips to each long edge of the crepe so that approximately ⅛in (2mm) of gold shows. Decorate about 8in (20cm) only along the edge as the rest will not show.

2

Roll the crepe around the tube with the gold edge showing. Secure it with double-sided tape. Twist one end of the crepe and tie and knot with gold thread. Fill the cracker with bonbons or a motto, then twist and tie the other end. For the band, photocopy a pretty flower image, cut to a 2¾ x 6in (7 x 15cm) rectangle and decorate the two longest sides with the scalloped edges from the gold doily paper as Step 1. Wrap this around the cracker, securing it with double-sided tape.

3

Cut out simple flower shapes from the tissue paper. Pierce the center of each flower with a darning needle. Using a 2in (5cm) length of floristry wire or a store-bought stem, turn over the top of the stem by about ⅛in (2mm). Gather three or four layers of petals together and thread on to the stem, positioning at the turned end. Fix in position with a spot of glue. When completely dry, pinch each flower slightly at the base to give it shape. Thread one under each floral band.

Beribboned Favor Bags

Materials

White Japanese
Kyoseishi paper

Grosgrain ribbon ⅜in (1cm)
or ⅝in (1.5cm) wide

Template on page 121

Cutting board

Craft knife

Metal safety ruler

Pencil

Bone folder

Scissors

Hole punch

Double-sided tape

Spray adhesive

The tradition of giving "favors" is a thoughtful way of thanking each guest for coming to celebrate your special day, and these pretty bags, cut and folded from pure-white textured paper, are so simple to make. Decorated with an array of ribbons and filled with tempting marzipan treats, they become either a welcoming token at each table setting, or a charming parting gift.

1

Using the template on page 121 as a guide, cut out the bag from the Kyoseishi paper, using pencil and ruler, cutting board, and craft knife. Working with the wrong side of the paper facing you, use the bone folder to score along the fold lines as marked on the template, folding toward you. Also crease the side pleats as marked on the template.

2

Glue along the vertical side flap, using double-sided tape on the right side of the paper to attach the sides of the bag. Carefully position the flap against the side seam of the bag and press the two sides together to fix. Now fold the base of the bag and glue the flaps with double-sided tape on the inside of the folds. Press into position to fix.

3

With scissors, cut a rectangle of Kyoseishi paper 2 x 4in (5 x 10cm). Glue one side with spray adhesive and press down firmly inside the base of the bag. Hold in position until dry. This will add extra firmness and help the bag hold its shape. At this point, crease the side pleats again to reinforce the shape of the bag.

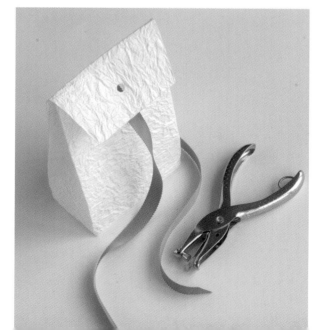

4

Fold over the top flap of the bag and use the hole punch to punch a hole ¾in (2cm) from the bottom edge of the flap and centered in the width, as marked on the template, making sure to punch the hole through all three thicknesses of paper. Fill the favor bags and close the flap, then thread a length of grosgrain ribbon through the holes and tie loosely at the front.

Beribboned Cones

These curvy cones are rolled from translucent and moiré papers and secured with overlong ribbons. The cones should be placed in a bowl with the ribbons trailing to each guest's place setting at the table.

Materials

230gsm Pergamenata or similar semi-transparent paper

Silver moiré patterned tissue paper

Thin white card

Template on page 120

40in (1m) lengths of a selection of 1cm (⅜in) wide grosgrain ribbons

Sample pots of matt emulsion paint in soft gray and blues

Artist's flat paintbrush

Pencil

Hole punch

Scissors

Extra-strength all-purpose adhesive

Spray adhesive

1

With scissors, cut out the oval-shaped cones to 9in (22cm) long from Pergamenata paper, using the template on page 120 as a guide. To decorate the ovals, paint around the edge with matt emulsion paint, which can be bought in small sample pots. Choose a paint color that matches the grosgrain ribbons.

2

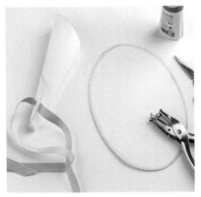

Punch a hole in the oval as indicated on the template. To make the cone, twist the oval into a cone shape so the punched hole is on the outside, bottom edge. Glue into position using extra-strength all-purpose adhesive, leaving the punched hole unglued. Hold in place until the glue has completely dried. Then thread a 40in (1m) length of ribbon through the hole and tie with a loose knot.

3

For an alternative colorway, cut out the oval shape in thin card and cover with a layer of silver moiré tissue paper, using spray adhesive to glue the two surfaces together. Form the cone as in Step 2 and thread with a matching ribbon. Now fill the cones with candy, jelly beans, or sugared almonds.

Memories Album

Preserve your memories by compiling an enchanting, ribbon-bound album to hold the precious keepsakes and mementos relating to your wedding day and the preparation time beforehand. A swatch of silk-satin, a sample of tulle, a faded flower—all find safe haven within interleaving glassine pages.

Materials

300gsm watercolor paper

150gsm watercolor paper

Thin white card

40gsm glassine paper

80in (2m) length of
1in (2.5cm) wide ivory ribbon

16½in (42cm) length of
⅜in (1cm) wide ivory ribbon

Decorative sheets of lettering
and vintage haberdashery

Cutting board

Craft knife

Metal safety ruler

Pencil

Scissors

Hole punch

Spray adhesive

Double-sided tape

Sample pots of matt emulsion
paint

Artist's flat paintbrush

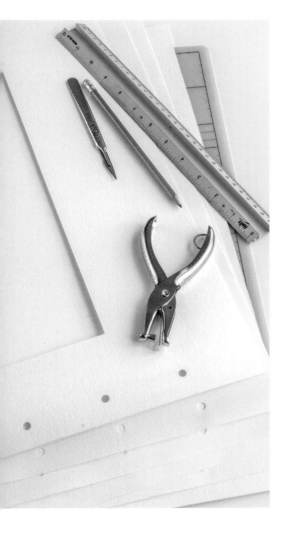

1

For the front and back album covers, use the pencil, ruler, craft knife, and cutting board to cut out two 12⅝ x 20in (32 x 50cm) rectangles from the 300gsm paper. Cut out a 4⅜ x 14⅛in (11 x 36cm) window centered visually on one of these rectangles. Cut out as many 12⅝ x 20in (32 x 50cm) pages from the 150gsm watercolor paper as you think you will need, remembering one of these will be used to back the "windowed" front cover. With the hole punch, make four holes along the spine ¾in (2cm) in from the edge, identically positioned on each page and the cover. Cut out the same number of pages 12⅝ x 18½in (32 x 46.5cm) from the glassine paper.

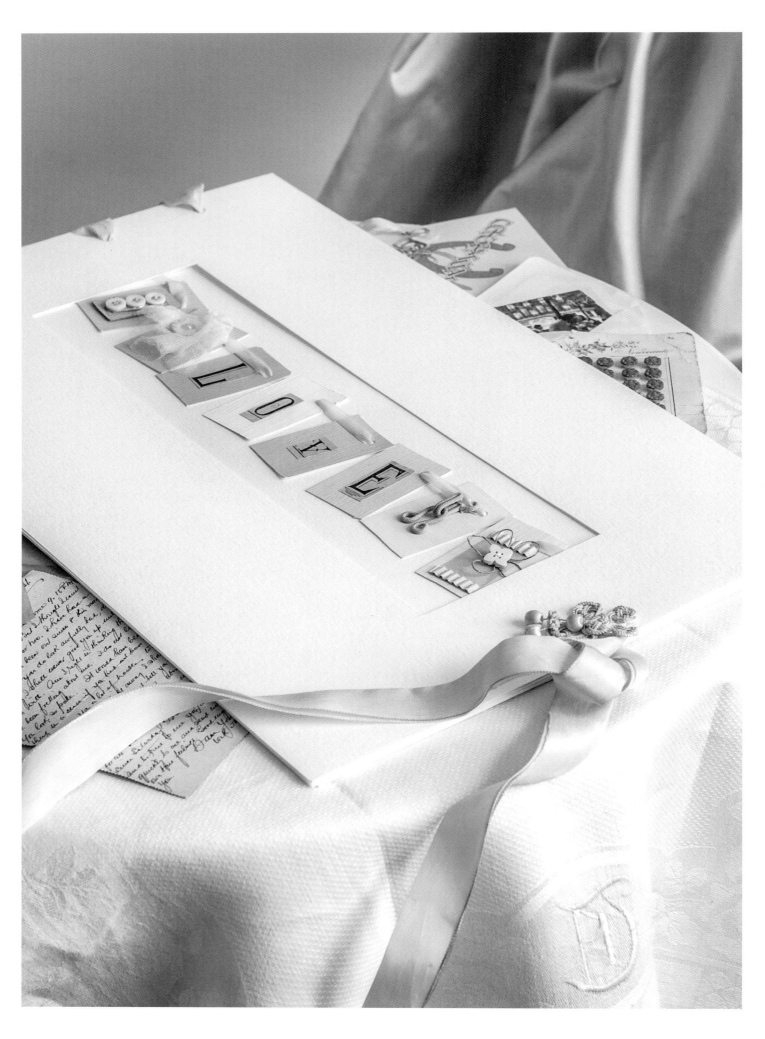

2

To decorate the front cover, paint eight rectangles in toning shades of emulsion paint on white card, each one at least 4 x 3⅛in (10 x 8cm). Alternatively, you can just buy colored card. When the paint is dry, cut eight 2⅜ x 1⅝in (6 x 4cm) rectangles from the painted card and punch a hole in each one, in the top right-hand corner. Decorate each card with a mixture of cut-out letters spelling the word LOVE, tiny buttons on a card, and a piece of lace or tulle, to make a creative collage. Fix in position with double-sided tape.

3

Thread thin ribbon loosely through the eight decorated cards. Place this chain on a page and frame it within the "windowed" cover. Glue the two ends of the ribbon and the cards in position with double-sided tape. Spray the wrong side of the "windowed" card using spray adhesive and glue it to the decorated page making sure the punch holes are aligned. For the fastening, stick 20in (50cm) of ribbon to the right-hand edge using double-sided tape. Repeat for the back fastening.

4

Interleave each page with a sheet of glassine, positioned 1⅜in (3.5cm) in from the spine edge, by spraying a ¼in (5mm) strip down the left-hand edge, masking off all other areas, and gluing in position; or use thin strips of double-sided tape. Assemble all the pages between the front and back cover so the holes align. Cut two 4in (10cm) lengths of ribbon, one for each of the two center holes. Pass each ribbon through a hole, overlap at the back, and fix with double-sided tape. For the "handle" cut 32in (80cm) of ribbon, pass 4in (10cm) through each outer hole, loop at the back, and stick with double-sided tape.

TIP Old, perhaps damaged, theater programs, song sheets, and magazines are invaluable for their decorative and unusual examples of lettering. The individual letters can be cut to form a word or phrase so that, when combined with new watercolor or other art paper and card, the faded charm of the typography takes on a contemporary look. These papers are often fragile so cut carefully with a craft knife or sharp scissors—if you are using the craft knife don't forget to secure the page to a cutting board with masking tape in order to keep in place as you cut.

Wish Tree

This lovely idea takes inspiration from a Dutch tradition. Pendants of watercolor paper, each lettered with a guest's name, are decorated with translucent and textured paper leaves threaded through ribbons and draped over a champagne glass to designate their place at the wedding table. Each person writes a wish to the bride and groom on the back of the pendant and ties it to a slender branch, so creating a striking display.

Materials

150gsm watercolor paper

88gsm Japanese Kyoseishi bleached white paper

21gsm Japanese Rakusui Lace Flocked paper tissue

Green silk paper

40gsm linen-look glassine paper

40gsm plain glassine paper

90 or 112gsm tracing paper

Templates on page 127

Selection of slender ribbons, 40in (1m) per pendant

Gold or silver marker pen (extra-fine point)

Hole punch

Cutting board

Craft knife

Metal safety ruler

Pencil

Scissors

Double-sided tape

Twigs and thin, contorted branches

Selection of thin glass vases

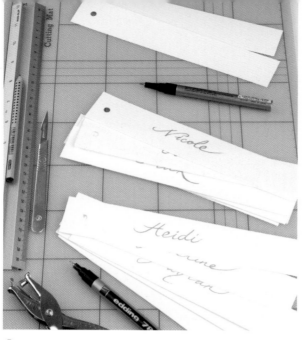

1

For the hanging pendants, with a ruler and pencil, cutting board, and craft knife, cut rectangles of watercolor paper 1⅝ x 8⅝in (4 x 22cm). Make a hole at one end with the hole punch, about ⅜in (1cm) in from the edge. Use a marker pen to write the name of a guest on one side of each of the rectangular pendants. Leave the other side blank for your guest to write a personal "wish" for the bride and groom.

2

Gather together a selection of white papers, mixing translucent papers with Kyoseishi textured paper. Include an accent color if required, in this case a green silk paper. With scissors or craft knife cut out the leaf shapes from the templates on page 127. Punch a hole at the base of each leaf about ⅜in (1cm) in from the end. Crease each leaf down its length, to give it extra form.

3

Select a mixture of four or five leaves for each cluster plus one pendant, then thread them together with ribbon. Tie a loose half-knot at the base of each cluster. Place one leaf and pendant cluster for each guest at the wedding table along with a silver pen so each person can write a "wish" on the back. The guest will then tie the "wish" to a branch of the wish tree with the ribbon. Make the wish tree by standing various twigs and slender branches, the more contorted the better, in a thin glass vase.

4

For an alternative color scheme, write the name of each guest with gold marker pen and choose soft pink, taupe, coffee, and ivory ribbons for each leaf cluster, making sure to use white leaves only.

TIP Translucent paper can create especially beautiful wedding decorations when you want to achieve a delicate and ethereal effect. You can use utility papers, such as glassine and tracing paper, as well as the decorative papers, such as Japanese Rakusui (with gaps on the surface created by dropping water) and Japanese Unryu (with embedded silk fibers). Thai silk papers, in beautiful jewel-like colors, are also useful. Fine papers are tricky to cut, especially with a craft knife, so try laying a firmer, opaque paper underneath. Secure with masking tape before you start.

Materials

10 x 14in (25.5 x 35.5cm) pad of 300gsm acrylic textured paper

⅛in (2mm) ivory mount board

Gray paper

40gsm clear glassine paper

Black and white photocopy of vintage postcard or wedding photograph

Tracing paper

12in (30cm) length of ⅞in (2.2cm) wide cotton or rayon tape

48in (1.2m) length of 1¼in (3cm) wide metallic ribbon

Diamanté brooch

Cutting board

Craft knife with fine blade no.11

Metal safety ruler

Pencil

Bone folder

Hole punch

Scissors

Spray adhesive

Double-sided tape

Masking tape

Photograph Album

Memories of the wedding day or honeymoon are relived in this captivating album, made of pages taken from a sketchbook rebound and decorated with silvery ribbon. An evocative image and a line of lettering enhance the cover and a moon-shaped diamanté brooch provides the final sparkling touch.

1

Remove the existing front and back covers of the acrylic pad leaving the inside pages. Cut out the same number of sheets of the glassine to 10 x 12in (25.5 x 30cm). Cut out a back cover from the mount board to 10 x 14in (25.5 x 35.5cm). Punch two holes in each textured paper page and in the back cover board 7⁄8in (2.3cm) in from the left-hand edge and 3⅜in (8.5cm) from the top and bottom. Mark 2in (5cm) in from the spine edge on all textured paper pages and using the bone folder against a ruler, score a fold line. Fold each page upward to form a flexible crease. Leaving two sheets aside for the cover, interleave each page with a sheet of glassine, using spray adhesive along a ¼in (5mm) strip, masking off all other areas. Position within the fold mark.

2

For the front cover decoration, use the black and white photocopy from a vintage postcard or favorite wedding photograph. Cut to a 6in (15cm) square. Visually center this on the front cover and mark out two slot marks that will hold each corner of the image, very lightly with pencil and ruler. Cut out slots using craft knife and cutting board.

3

Insert the image into the slots. Spray the back of this page with spray adhesive and glue to another page, aligning the holes. You may have to spray quite heavily as the textured paper tends to absorb the adhesive. This now forms the front cover and the image is held securely in place.

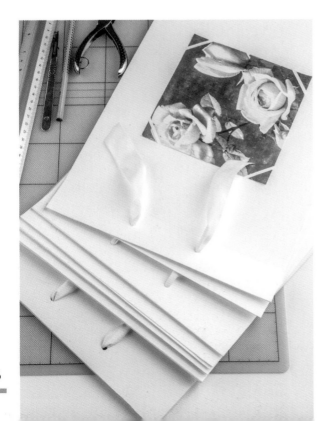

4

Assemble all the pages between the front and back covers, aligning the holes, and then thread the length of cotton tape through the holes. Tie the ends of the cotton tape together tightly at the front with as flat a knot as possible and trim off the ends with scissors.

5

Key the word "photos" into the computer using an italic script typeface—French Script has been used here—and print it out. Trace the lettering and transfer to a small sheet of gray paper. Fix the paper to the cutting board with masking tape and cut out the lettering carefully with a craft knife or scissors.

6

Wrap metallic ribbon around the album, covering the cotton tape. Secure at the back with double-sided tape. For a flat bow, cut a 16in (40cm) length of ribbon. Fold each end into the middle and stick with double-sided tape. Wrap a shorter piece around the join, secure with double-sided tape. Attach the bow to the ribbon in the same way and add a diamanté brooch. Glue the lettering to the cover using some spray adhesive.

TIP A collection of evocative sepia or black and white imagery found on old postcards (or perhaps even your own contemporary snapshots) is always inspirational. These can be photocopied and enlarged so the detail is seen afresh to stunning effect. Don't forget to use a paper other than the standard photocopying paper for a more subtle effect. Antique "paste" buckles, brooches, and clasps, and glamorous vintage costume jewelry are fascinating to collect and can be picked up easily at antique fairs and bric-a-brac markets. From delicate marcasite to dazzling diamanté, all combine beautifully with a monochrome color palette.

Thank-you Folder

Personalize your thank-you notes, adding your own indelible style, with these simple tracing paper folders embellished with a rose cluster motif, a vintage glass button, and entwined gold thread. Each folder is lined with semi-translucent pages and contains a sweet matching envelope to hold a few thoughtful keepsakes and a handwritten note.

Materials

Color photocopies on 60gsm A4 tracing paper

90gsm Pergamenata or semi-translucent paper

Ivory "laid" paper

Decorative images and photographs

Vintage gold thread

Vintage glass buttons

Template on page 126

Cutting board

Craft knife

Metal safety ruler

Pencil

Bone folder

Scissors

Spray adhesive

Multi-purpose adhesive

Double-sided tape

Fountain pen and black ink

1

Choose a favorite floral image, perhaps from a vintage postcard, and photocopy it onto an A4 sheet of tracing paper, positioning the floral design at one end of the paper so that it will appear on the front cover of the folder when folded in half. For the inner lining pages, cut the Pergamenata paper to 8¼ x 11½in (21 x 29.7cm) using pencil, ruler, craft knife, and cutting board.

2

Fold the photocopied tracing papers in half to 8¼ x 5¾in (21 x 14.8cm). Repeat this with the semi-translucent paper using a bone folder as this paper is of a heavier weight. Glue the lining inside the tracing-paper folder with spray adhesive by spraying ¼in (5mm) along the back fold of semi-translucent paper, masking off all other areas, then press to adhere against the spine. For the fastening, glue a glass button at the front using a spot of the multi-purpose adhesive. Cut a 48in (120cm) length of the gold thread for the fastening.

3

Using the template on page 126 cut out an envelope from the semi-translucent paper to a length of 13½in (33.5cm) using a cutting board and craft knife. With the wrong side of the paper facing you, use the bone folder to crease the fold marks as indicated on the template.

4

Cover the right sides of the two side flaps with the spray adhesive, first being careful to mask off the surrounding areas. Fold the bottom flap upward, positioning over the side flaps, to form the envelope. Cut a 4in (10cm) length of gold thread, fold it in two, and knot the ends together to form a loop. Attach it in the center of the top edge using a spot of multi-purpose glue. Glue a glass button to the "pocket" of the envelope in a position to take the loop of thread when the top flap of the envelope is folded over.

5

Write your "thank-you" message with fountain pen and black ink on a 3½ x 4⅜in (9 x 11cm) sheet of "laid" paper. Insert this vertically into the pocket along with a decorative card and photo. Fasten the loop around the button, place into the folder, and fix with a piece of double-sided tape. Fold the thread in half and loop the folded end around the glass button, wrap the two ends around the folder and then several times around the button to fasten securely.

Templates

Here are all the templates you'll need for the projects in this book. Actual-size templates can be traced off the page. Others will need to be enlarged on a photocopier to the given percentage.

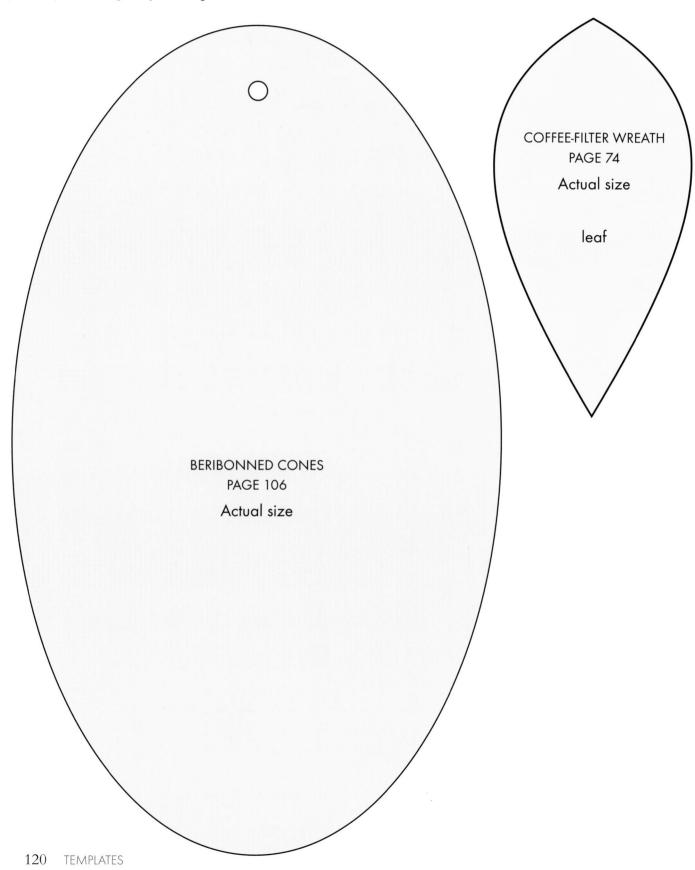

COFFEE-FILTER WREATH
PAGE 74

Actual size

leaf

BERIBONNED CONES
PAGE 106

Actual size

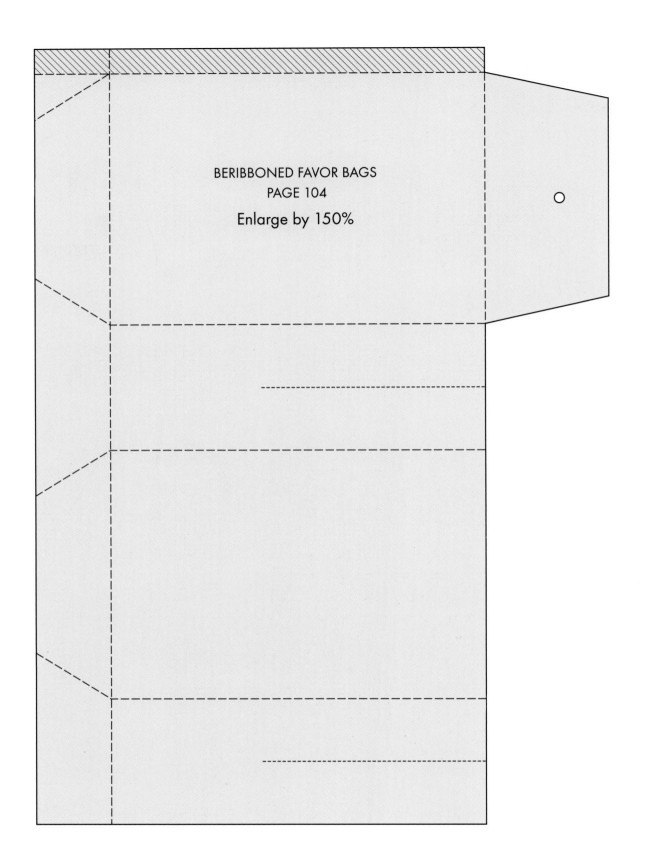

BERIBBONED FAVOR BAGS
PAGE 104

Enlarge by 150%

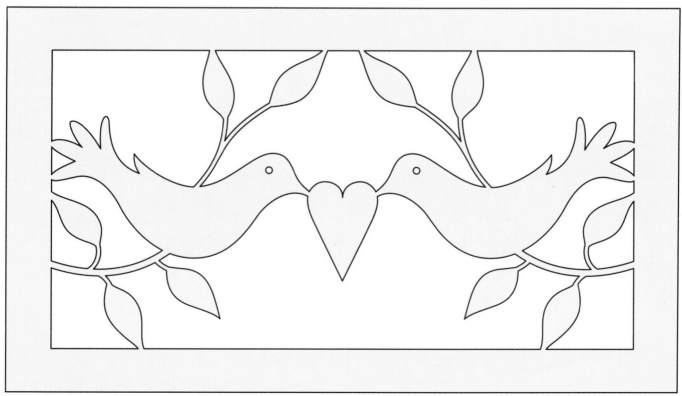

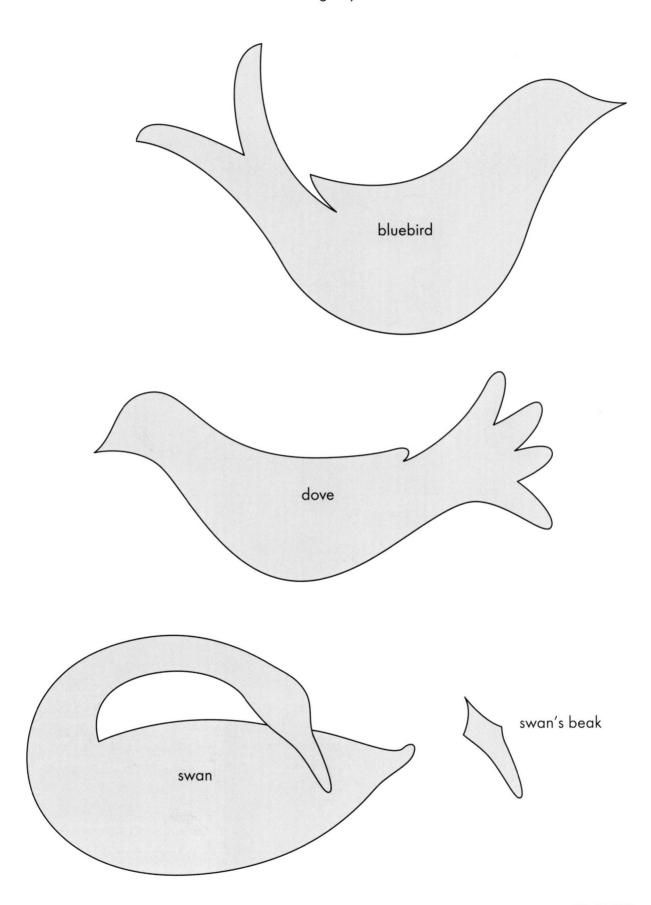

bluebird

dove

swan

swan's beak

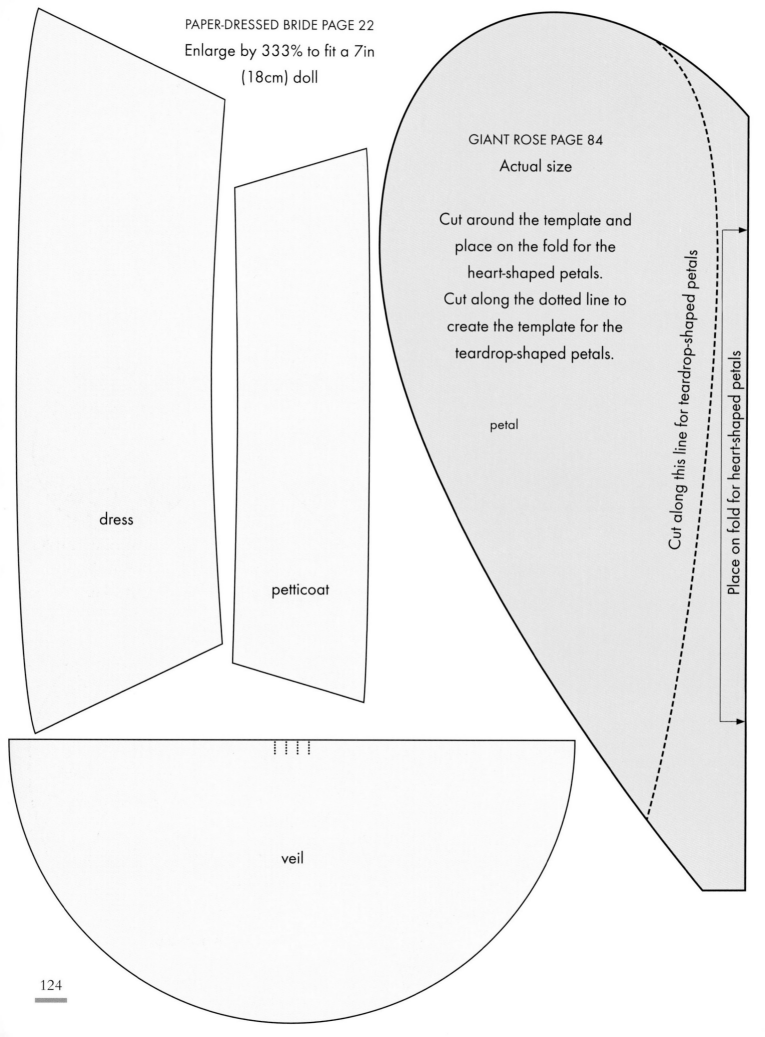

GIANT ROSE PAGE 84

Actual size

Cut around the template and
place on the fold for the
heart-shaped petals.
Cut along the dotted line to
create the template for the
teardrop-shaped petals.

petal

dress

petticoat

veil

Cut along this line for teardrop-shaped petals

Place on fold for heart-shaped petals

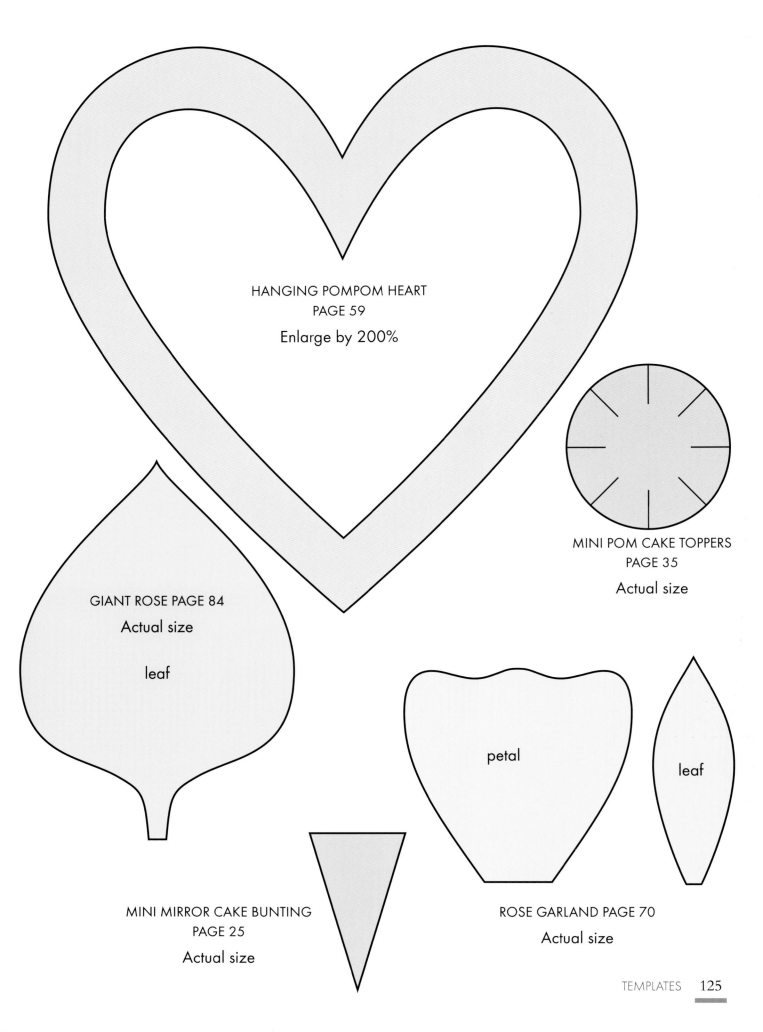

HANGING POMPOM HEART
PAGE 59

Enlarge by 200%

MINI POM CAKE TOPPERS
PAGE 35

Actual size

GIANT ROSE PAGE 84
Actual size

leaf

petal

leaf

MINI MIRROR CAKE BUNTING
PAGE 25

Actual size

ROSE GARLAND PAGE 70

Actual size

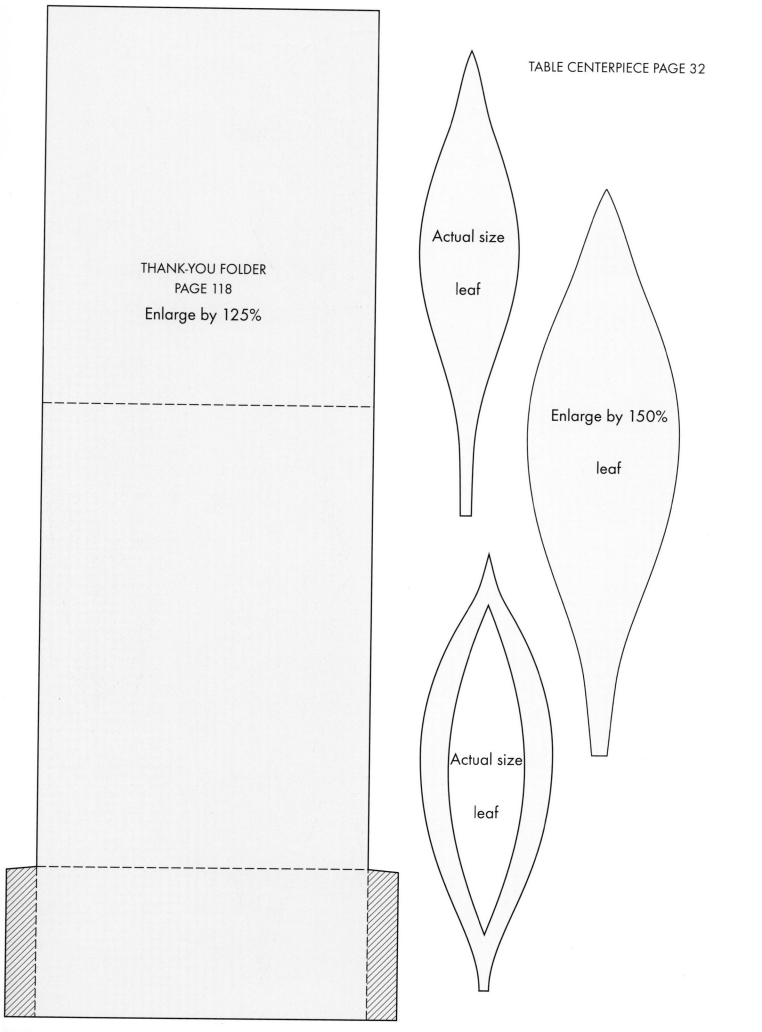

THANK-YOU FOLDER
PAGE 118
Enlarge by 125%

TABLE CENTERPIECE PAGE 32

Actual size

leaf

Enlarge by 150%

leaf

Actual size

leaf

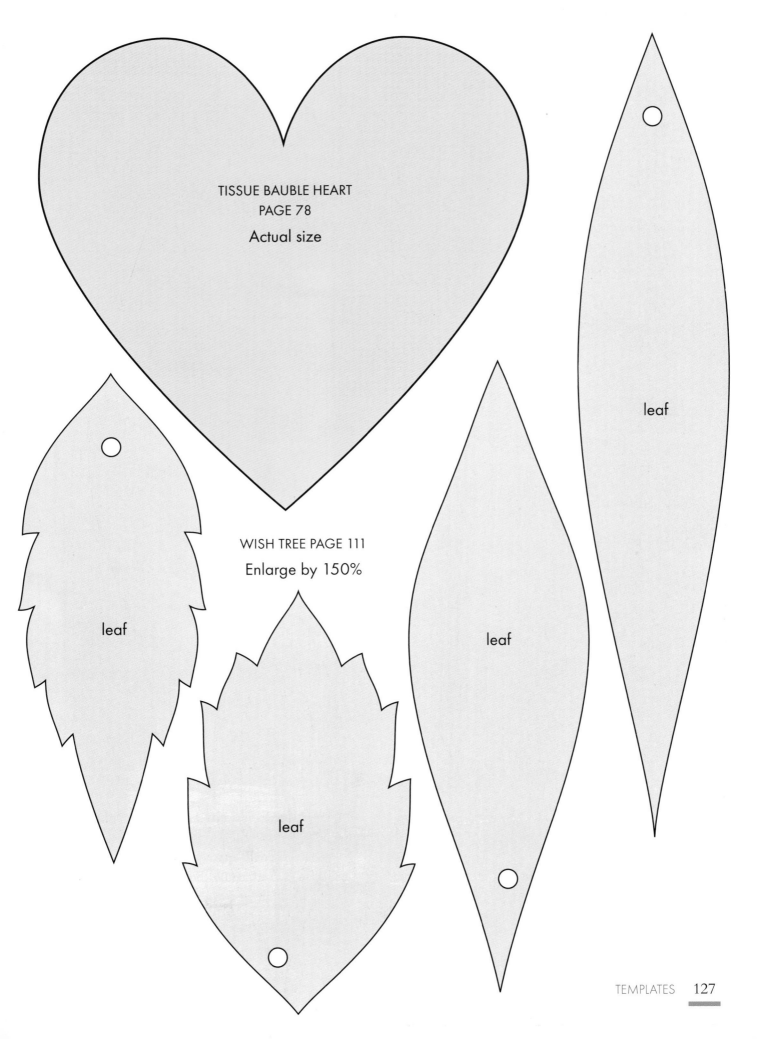

TISSUE BAUBLE HEART
PAGE 78

Actual size

leaf

WISH TREE PAGE 111
Enlarge by 150%

leaf

leaf

leaf

leaf

Index

Suppliers

USA AND CANADA

A C Moore
www.acmoore.com

Hobby Lobby
www.hobbylobby.com

Jo-ann Fabric & Crafts
www.joann.com

Michaels
www.michaels.com

UK

Hobbycraft
www.hobbycraft.co.uk

John Lewis
www.johnlewis.co.uk